The Bargain Hunter's Handbook

How to Buy
Just About Anything
for Next to Nothing

The Bargain Hunter's Handbook

How to Buy Just About Anything for Next to Nothing

By Rob and Terry Adams

GALAHAD BOOKS
NEW YORK

First Galahad Books edition published in 2003.

Galahad Books
A division of BBS Publishing Corporation
450 Raritan Center Parkway
Edison, NJ 08837

Galahad Books is a registered trademark of BBS Publishing Corporation

Published by arrangement with The Career Press, Inc.

Distributed by Sterling Publishing Company, Inc.
387 Park Avenue South
New York, NY 10016

Distributed in Canada by Sterling Publishing
Canadian Manda Group
One Atlantic Avenue, Suite 105
Toronto, Ontario, Canada M6K3E7

Distribution in Australia by Capricorn Link (Australia) Pty, Ltd.
PO Box 704
Windsor NSW 2756 Australia

ISBN: 1-57866-112-9

Printed in the United States of America.

Dedication

This one's for Tim,
who really knew how to have fun in a superstore.

Acknowledgments

We could not have made this book what it is without the wonderful assistance of a lot of terrific people, including: the savvy bargain hunters who shared their shopping secrets with us, Sheila Bankhead and her excellent reference team at the downtown Panama City branch of the Bay County Public Library, and Cliff, Matt, Big Al, Barney, Susan, Leo, David and Vivian at our favorite home improvement store. Thanks, gang!

Contents

INTRODUCTION Seekers of the Hidden Bargain

Most people have no idea that great bargains surround them as they meander through aisles of merchandise. Searching only for the red letters that announce "sale," they never realize they can create their own discounts.

Mention "bargain" to the average shopper and you conjure up visions of outlet malls, discount centers, and department store basements. But the true bargain-hunter—an archaeologist/adventurer of another kind—knows the many mysteries hidden within the hearts and stockrooms of regular retailers, and what's more, knows how to unearth them.

Real bargain-hunting is an art, a quest, and a game. It's spotting a sale before it's official. Sniffing out a deal that doesn't yet exist. Creating bargains where most people see unmarked merchandise.

Bargain-hunting is a terrific way to stretch your purchasing dollar. Suddenly, you'll find you can afford those extra amenities. You can remodel your house, refurnish your apartment, put a set of snazzy wheels in your driveway, obtain new electronic gizmos at your fingertips, and give splashy gifts—all while keeping well within your monetary means.

Bargain-hunting is also a heck of a lot of fun, as irresistible as caffeine or chocolate, and less stress on your nerves and waistline. It's cheap entertainment. Shopping with a strategy. Shopping with panache. Shopping with a vengeance. Your new motto: I shop 'til you drop your price.

Okay, you say: When can I start? You did, the moment you picked up this book.

12 secrets of the bargain-seeker

The world is brimming with bargains and places to find them. We'll explore them all as we wend through this book. But no matter where you go, whatever bargain you're hunting, you'll use the same set of secrets.

You don't have to spend hours memorizing these strategies, or do all your shopping with your nose stuck in this book, anxiously thumbing through dog-eared pages. These secrets employ simple, common-sense techniques that will quickly become second-nature. They're civilized, courteous, and resourceful. And they'll take you everywhere you want to go, on every shopping adventure. Once you've mastered them, you can bargain with the best.

Ready? Here we go!

Secret 1 - Don't be shy

The bottom line of bargaining is haggling, or, if you prefer, discussing the price: what the merchant is willing to take versus what you're willing to spend. The word *bargain*, by way of Middle French and then English, stems from the ancient Latin term, *barcaniare*, for trade. And that's actually what bargaining is: a fair trade. You're trading your cash (or charge card) for the seller's products. But you're also trading in less tangible assets. You're giving the seller the opportunity to move merchandise—goods that cost him money sitting on the shelf—and, of course, you're giving him a valuable sales ally for the future: you!

The average shopper is too faint-hearted to haggle. But most retailers, from superstore department managers to mom-and-pop operators, are surprisingly receptive.

Why? Retailers live in a store-eat-store world. They know that if you don't buy a product from them, you'll buy it from the competition. And they also know that if you walk out their doors, there's an excellent chance you won't come back. Therefore, they're motivated to sell to you while you're still their captive audience.

And with good reason. Merchandise collecting dust on store shelves costs retailers money in more ways than one. Shoppers want to see and touch the latest model and the latest fashion, in everything from clothing to carpets to commodes. Stock still on display leaves no room for the next generation of product—the stuff that matches or beats the competition's wares. Merchandise still clogging the aisles gives corporate management the unpleasant idea that the store isn't generating much business.

So it's in the store manager's—and his department managers'—best interests to get rid of everything that's not fresh off the distributor's truck. The secret here is that retailers—no dummies—won't tell you they're anxious to see the last of this stuff. You have to nose around. You have to ask. And while there's no need to be bombastic, you certainly don't want to be shy. Remember: Bargain-hunting is an adventure!

Marks the Spot

The sidewalk sale is the retail store's version of the yard or garage sale. You'll often find all sorts of fascinating clearance items here. These informal sales are bargain hot spots because the last thing the employees want to do is drag everything back inside at the end of the day.

Secret 2 - Present a logical reason for the seller to discount

Despite the fact that retailers are secretly anxious to sell, they're not simply going to hand over the store. You have to give them a reason or incentive to discount to you. Sometimes that incentive is cash. Sometimes it's buying all they have of a

B A R G A I N H U N T E R ' S J O U R N A L

• The last laugh •

We found two boxes of doorknobs, 12 in a box, at a home improvement store's sidewalk sale. Not just any doorknobs, but the old-fashioned faceted glass type they just don't seem to make any more, along with the polished brass latches and back plates to go with them. We'd been searching for some of this stuff for years. Grabbing up the boxes before somebody else discovered them, we sought out Shelly, the department manager. "How much do you want for these?" Rob asked.

It was a freezing February morning. Shelly peered at the jumble of glass and metal, shivering inside her parka. "I'd have to take $20 a box."

"You've got an awful lot of stuff to get rid of," Rob countered. "How about $20 for both boxes?" Shelly pursed her lips, and reluctantly agreed.

The knobs would add just the right touch to a collection of old Florida cottages we were renovating and we'd paid less than one-tenth of what they were worth. But we weren't the only happy ones. As we left the sale, we caught Shelly exchanging high fives with a co-worker. "You know those old boxes of doorknobs? I finally got rid of them!"

certain item. Sometimes it's just the fact that (to paraphrase Arnold Schwarzenegger) you'll be back. Get creative. If you can't think of a reason, make one up. If nothing else, you'll have a good chuckle and so, hopefully, will the seller.

Here are the quintessential bargain hunter's reasons to discount, followed by a sample "icebreaker." You can use the lines as presented, or ad lib in whatever way suits your personality and situation:

- *Overstocks.* "I see you're a little overstocked here on widgets. How much would you discount one of them for? What if I bought them all?"

- *Overabundance of floor models.* "I notice you have two floor models. How would you feel about discounting one?"

- *Merchandise missing packaging.* Perfectly fine, but devoid of a box because it was either a display item or fell prey to a previous shopper's curiosity. "Say, what about that widget over there that's not in a box? How much would you take for it?"

- *Imperfect merchandise.* "This television has a scratch along the side. How much can you give me off it?" (No need to mention that you plan to put the TV in an entertainment center where the entire scratched side will be hidden from view).

- *Not the newest model.* "This computer is a 333 Mhz system, and all the new ones are 366 or 400. What's the best you can do for me on it?"

- *Not the right season.* "The weather's getting awfully cold for barbecuing and I see that's your last gas grill. Can you lower the price on it?"

- *Cash.* This works better with small business retailers or private party transactions than with chain stores that have to report to somebody else. The attraction for the independent seller is that he doesn't have to worry that your check might bounce, he doesn't have to wait for it to clear, and he doesn't have to pay the extra percentage charged him by credit card companies. "I see you're asking $50 for that item. Could you take $40 for it if I paid cash?"

• *Return business.* "In my business, I always need widgets. If you can get the price down for me, I'll be in here a lot to buy more."

◤reasure Chest Trivia

The top three retailers in 1997, according to both the National Retail Federation's magazine *Stores* and American Express, were Wal-Mart, Sears, and Kmart.

Secret 3 - Don't get attached

This secret's often the most difficult to adhere to. It can also be the most important. Whatever it is you want to buy, don't want it so badly that you lose your ability to bargain. Once the seller sees that you must have his product, he knows he's got you hooked and he loses his incentive to come down in price.

So dull that gleam in your eye. Even though the item might be exactly what you want in every way, shape, and form, act nonchalant. If the salesman asks why you're drooling, say you haven't had lunch yet.

If you know yourself, and you know you'll have a hard time not waxing rhapsodic over a particular object, bring a friend. Study old *Law and Order* episodes and perform the bargain-hunting version of good cop/bad cop. Say you're shopping

B A R G A I N H U N T E R ' S J O U R N A L

• Extreme vanity •

While strolling through the building supply store, we came across a gorgeous solid oak vanity cabinet. It featured an unusual 5-foot length and seemed to have been custom-made for our master bathroom, which had been built in a sort of 80s minimalist style. With four roomy drawers, arched doors, and brass pulls, the cabinet was perfect except for the kick plate and one side which seemed to have met with an unfortunate accident involving a forklift. The store manager had reduced the piece $100 from the original $400 sticker price.

We wanted that vanity. The damaged side could be removed, since it would sit flush against our bathroom wall, and all the kick plate needed was to be reattached with a couple of screws. But it wasn't a bargain. Yet.

The next week, the vanity had been reduced an additional $100—now it was half price. We approached Clint, the department manager, and offered him $40. He suggested we come back on Friday. When we returned on that afternoon, he flashed us a grin and said, "Get that thing out of here."

We did. And it looks terrific in our bathroom.

for a sofa and you find one you adore. You blurt out that the color is perfect for your living room. The salesman gets excited—he smells a sale. Your partner counters that the sofa might be too big for your space. The salesman, fearing a lost commission, swings into negotiation mode.

But you're still blinded by love. You exclaim that the sofa's classic lines match the rest of your décor and your dog will like the cushy pillows. The salesman gets excited again. Your bad cop partner immediately points out that it's more money than you had planned on spending. And the salesman goes back on bargain alert.

After your friend kicks you in the shin, you wise up and get with the program. You walk away and look at something less expensive. "Well," you say, "if that first sofa we looked at was priced like this one, I might go for it." You still want the one with the cushy pillows, but don't show it. And you let the bargaining begin.

Secret 4 - Make buddies, and make yourself available

Get to know the folks who run the stores you frequent. As you cruise the aisles, keep your eyes open for familiar faces. Find out who's who: the department managers, the store manager, and especially the sharper associates, who know what's really going on in the store—what and where the bargains are. They're the people who either have the power to discount, or the ambition to take your discount request to someone who can approve it.

Salespeople are not store servants—they're potential allies. Find out their names and ask for them the next time you visit the store. This secret has an additional bonus: You develop a rapport with the salesperson you've asked for, but you also begin a rapport with his co-workers. His colleagues will notice that you're asking for him and he will make it their business to find out why. When the salesperson discovers that you're a good customer for his own department's special sales, he'll give you a call.

Reward your store allies. Many stores give bonuses or brownie points to employees for customer service. When one of your sources gives you a good deal, call or write to the store manager and tell him how much you appreciated the salesperson's extra attention—it's why you shop there. Besides being a nice gesture, it gives your buddy one more reason to remember you.

E xpedition Tip

Once you've established yourself as a bargain hunter with your sales allies, the very sight of you in the store will often set visions of special sale items (or as we call them, "must-goes") dancing through their heads—special items that they'll pass on to you.

Secret 5 – You gotta shop around

You can't know what a good deal is until you know what it isn't. Be your own *"Consumer Reports"*: get out there and investigate whatever it is you want to buy. Research as many makes and models as possible, especially when pursuing big-ticket items. See which equipment has the features you must have and then decide which ones you can live without. At the same time, compare prices between models and between stores. Find out when the next generation, or next model, is expected to arrive because that's when prices on the current models will drop—sometimes drastically.

Don't dump everything and decide you've got to have a new freezer today, unless it's August and ice cream is puddling in the bottom of your current model. You'll do much better when you give yourself time to shop around. Instead of pressuring yourself or your significant other to make a buying decision immediately, make your rounds. Visit your sales allies and put them on the lookout for your dream item. At the same time, explore other areas—stores you haven't previously visited, mail-order catalogs, the Internet. Then when you track down that terrific bargain, you'll know it's a great deal.

T reasure Chest Trivia

According to the U.S. Energy Information Administration, more than 77 percent of American households boast a washing machine, but only 50.2 percent have a dishwasher (unless you count the human kind).

Secret 6 – Show that your intentions are serious

Sellers are much more interested in buyers than in browsers and therefore more motivated to bargain. So once again, get out there and get nosy. Ask questions about the product. Demonstrate the research you've already done. For example, if you're hunting a dishwasher, ask about features like cycles, noise level, water usage, and rust-free interior parts. This tells the salesperson that you know what you want, you're informed about the merchandise—possibly because you've just come from the competition down the street—and you're serious about buying.

This motivates him to take you seriously, and to take your bargain-seeking seriously as well. He doesn't want you taking your brilliance (and your bucks) somewhere else.

Once you've made that purchase, remember that you've also made a friend in the business. Seek out your new buddy the next time you're in the store. Let him know how much you're enjoying your item and how much you appreciate the deal he gave you. And every time you're in the store, even if you don't need anything in that department, stop in and say a friendly "Hey!" Ask if anything special is coming up. Keep the lines of communication open.

Secret 7 - Be willing to walk away

If the seller doesn't accept your offer and won't compromise, walk away. Sometimes this is what it takes to get that great deal. As the old cliché goes, the grass is always greener on the other side—the other side being your retreating backside. Once the seller sees you heading into the sunset, he's already wishing he'd changed his mind. And if you walk slowly enough, he often will.

◆ reasure Chest Trivia

The top three specialty stores for 1997 were Toys "R" Us, Limited, and Circuit City, according to the National Retail Federation's *Stores* magazine and American Express.

Secret 8 - Be willing to walk back

Sometimes you have to walk back to give the seller a chance to change his mind. You're not losing face—you're keeping negotiations open and showing the seller you think enough of him and his product to want to return. Think back to your own experiences in selling a car or a house. Haven't there been times when you wished you hadn't been so quick to turn down an offer? That you wished the potential buyer would walk back through your door? Well, here's your opportunity to make someone else's dream come true.

Sometimes another day of sitting on a piece of unsold merchandise that hasn't sold is enough to get the seller to rethink your offer. Sometimes it's a few days or even a month. Occasionally, it can be a matter of moments.

We walked into our local home improvement superstore one sunny Sunday afternoon to buy a garden hose—and came out with a 31-inch TV for half the price. The TV was a floor model, the store was about to close down before moving to a new location, and the department manager was not looking forward to lugging the set across town. He'd already marked it down to $600 from the regular retail price of $800.

We offered $350. Bud, the manager, shook his head. "If I sold it to you for that price," he said, "I'd have half the employees in here trying to kill me because I didn't offer it to them first." Then he gave the TV another glance. He really didn't want the dang thing. "Okay," he said finally, "I'll give it to you for $450."

Bud said that was the best he could do. Unfortunately, it was more than we wanted to spend. And since we hadn't come into the store for a TV in the first place, we thanked him for his time, took our garden hose, and walked out. Halfway through the parking lot, we suddenly had a brainstorm.

We ditched the hose in the car, scuttled back into the store, and offered Bud his $450—if he could include the tax in that price. Bud got out his calculator, reverse engineered a sale price of about $420, and we went home with a new TV.

B A R G A I N H U N T E R ' S J O U R N A L

• Mercedes magic •

On our jaunts through town over the course of a recent holiday season, we spotted a spiffy little Mercedes SL convertible sitting in a small used-car dealership. Two weeks before Christmas and counting, the Mercedes was still there, along with every other car on the lot. It was reasonably priced, but we figured we could do better. Few people are interested in buying a car right before Christmas (how well will it fit under the tree?) and no one is interested in buying a convertible. Who wants to cruise with the top down when the weather's in the 30s?

Because the dealer was alone, with no manager or owner to have to satisfy, we figured he was approachable, and probably anxious to make a sale. We looked it over and in a pleasant way pointed out that the ragtop was ratty and the passenger's seatbelt was missing. We offered him 40 percent less than he was asking. He politely declined.

As we climbed into our own jalopy and drove off, we saw, in our rearview mirror, the man wildly waving our card. He accepted our offer, and we took home a terrific Christmas gift, even if it didn't fit under the tree.

Expedition Tip

Take the peaks and valleys of the salesperson's day into consideration when you're bargaining. If it's a hectic Saturday afternoon, he's surrounded by harried shoppers with too much to do and the store paging system is bellowing his name, let him know *briefly* what you're interested in and come back another day. He'll appreciate you for it—and you'll get a better deal.

Secret 9 - Don't insult and don't get insulted

Take this from Rob, a man who once got thrown out of a junk yard for insulting the merchandise. Bargaining is a friendly process. It's sounding out the seller and letting him sound you out. Once you get a sense of where each of you is coming from—and trying to go—you can make your offer. It can be a shade shy of the retail price or it can be ridiculously low.

But it should never be offered in an insulting manner. This is not the way to win friends or influence people. No one is going to cut you a better deal because you offended them, and no one is going to welcome you back or call you with a special deal because you scorned his wares.

If you suggest a discount on the grounds that a product is flawed, don't ever say something like, "How much would you take for that ratty old dresser with the missing drawer pulls?" Even in a second-hand store, you're insulting the seller. Instead, you'll want to word it along the lines of, "This is a great dresser, but the drawer pulls are missing. It's going to cost me X dollars to replace them. Can you give me Y off the price?"

While you're taking care not to insult the seller, make sure that you don't get your feelings hurt, either. Eventually, you're going to catch somebody on a day when everything's gone wrong and your bargain offer comes as the straw that breaks the seller's back. Don't take it personally. Chances are that the next time you encounter that seller, he'll be delighted to work with you.

Secret 10 - Find out the seller's mark-up

As you make friends in the retail world, seek out markups—the difference between what the product sells for and what the merchant paid for it. The reason? Unless it's a desperate situation, the seller isn't likely to let go of his merchandise for less than his cost. Knowing the mark-up gives you a handle on how much bargaining room you've got—and gives you that bargain hunter's rush when you come across a really great deal.

Keep in mind that the mark-ups your sales buddies are working with will vary, depending on factors such as the kind of deals they got for the goods.

Additionally, the mark-ups for private party merchandise can veer all over the place. That's why it's important for you to do your own research.

Again, don't worry about being nosy. Most people appreciate a healthy interest in their products, especially when they see that you're working toward making them an offer.

Some typical icebreakers:

- What's the store's cost for this particular item?
- This is a terrific item. Do you remember what you paid for it?
- I understand there's not a lot of markup on widgets. What is your profit margin?

The magic mark-up

There is no one magic mark-up for any retail sector, no single percentage that you can figure into every deal. It all depends on what the retailer paid for his goods and how much in the way of savings he wants to pass along to the average customer. That's why it's important to research and obtain all of the necessary information.

B A R G A I N H U N T E R ' S J O U R N A L

• Keep that hall tree •

When our friend Judy Anderson was a young married woman in Savannah, Georgia, her husband suggested they look at an antique brass bed that he'd seen advertised. Judy felt that her husband really wanted a brass bed, so she agreed to look. The first thing she saw when they walked in the door was a beautiful oak-and-brass hall tree.

"I fell in love with that hall tree," Judy says. "My heart was beating so fast I was afraid the elderly lady who owned the house would see it practically pounding out of my chest."

Then Judy fell for an oak armoire and a gorgeous carved oak bedroom set. She knew that this was a one-in-a-million opportunity. The seller was anxious to get rid of everything and Judy realized that the more she bought, the better price she'd get. She told her husband he could have the brass bed if the woman would sell the other pieces—including the hall tree—as well.

The woman obliged, and now the antiques have become a treasured feature of Judy's home. She says she's frequently asked to sell the hall tree (for big money, too), but, "I wouldn't sell it for anything. It's priceless to me."

There are industry norms, mark-ups that more or less hold true across the boards. Oriental rug dealers, for instance, mark up their merchandise so that after they give you a 50 percent discount, they still have between 30 percent and 50 percent profit left in the piece. Standard model major appliances, on the other hand, typically are marked up only about 15 percent. But deluxe models—refrigerators with the icemaker, water dispenser, and mood lighting in the door— carry higher mark-ups of up to 30 percent.

Electronics and small appliances such as microwaves and toasters also get marked up about 30 percent, while knickknacks and giftware can zoom up 150 percent. If you want to sit down and mull this over, you'll do so on furniture that carries a 55-percent mark up.

Secret 11 – Strike when the deal is hot

This one is the reverse face of the shop-around secret. Doing research before you buy is an excellent strategy, but every once in a while a really fabulous deal comes up, usually when you least expect it, and bites you in the backside. When that happens, you've got to be ready to jump—like shopping for a garden hose and coming out with a television.

We weren't looking for a TV at the time, but because we'd nosed around the electronics departments just for fun (doing research for ourselves), we recognized the TV as a terrific bargain. And we knew our old set was about ready for the Great Electronic Afterlife. So when the deal jumped up and bit us, we bit back.

If we'd waited until our old set coughed out its last commercial, the terrific TV would have been long gone, snapped up by some other savvy shopper or store employee.

This is not to advise, of course, that you should run around town with money burning a hole in your back pocket, ready to buy every piece of merchandise that makes eyes at you. Savvy bargain-seekers are shopping adventurers, but they're responsible, informed ones. Some deals you have to let slip through your fingers. No bargain is terrific if it's a strain on your budget or you simply don't need it.

Look at the unattainable deal this way. If it doesn't fit your pocketbook now, another (maybe even better) one will show up later after you've smartly saved your pennies on more affordable bargains.

And in the meantime, like die-hard fishermen, you can recount stories of "the one that got away."

◆ reasure Chest Trivia

If you're between the ages of 45 and 54, get ready to be depressed: You spend more money on just about every type of entertainment purchase than any other age group, according to a recent survey by the U.S. Bureau of Labor Statistics.

Secret 12 - Let in a little serendipity

One of the finer aspects of bargain-hunting is that, after a while, bargains seem to find you. You get a reputation for having that magic touch, the one that attracts unbelievable deals and incites healthy envy among your peers. It is magic—it stems from your ability to see every shopping experience as a potential bargain, and to recognize the truly outstanding ones when they come along. It also has something to do with your sense of adventure. Bargain-hunting, like life, pays unexpected dividends when you open yourself up to them.

The savvy bargain seeker leaves plenty of room for serendipity. Keep your eyes and ears open, your sense of humor honed, your bargaining antennae tuned, and you'll find those terrific deals in even the most unexpected places.

CHAPTER ONE Hidden Treasure

I f you've read this far you know that retail stores have a lot more for sale than what you see on the display floor. And you know that just because the shop doesn't have a big sign in the window that says "sale" doesn't mean there isn't anything *on* sale. But did you know that the very best buys, the ones that make the bargain hunter's heart soar, aren't advertised inside the store either?

It's true. The best stuff isn't advertised in the newspaper, it doesn't carry a sale sticker, and it may not even be out among the merchandise. Follow along with us in this chapter as we unlock the hidden treasures behind the retail veil.

Unadvertised booty

Stores often have perfectly good merchandise that they want to move but haven't promoted, either because the advertised sale won't start for several days or because they only have a few of each item. You'll find these gems stacked in the aisle, crowded near the front door, or even at the curb. Sometimes they're simply tucked on the shelf with a discreet mark-down sticker attached.

Well, if all those things are overflowing into the aisles or falling out the front door, why is it that nobody knows they're on sale? The answer, dear reader, is that most people aren't bargain hunters. They perceive a jumble of products as just that. They never take a second glance. It doesn't occur to them to ask what all that stuff is.

Of course, as a bargain hunter, you will do just that. You'll learn that it's a) merchandise that's being tagged for an upcoming sale,

b) merchandise that's being taken off the shelves because it didn't sell, or c) brand-new products that have just come in and haven't yet been put on the shelves.

If the answer is *a*, you're in the right place at the right time! You can have your pick today of whatever will be tomorrow's store special. If it's *b*, you're still in the right place because now is your chance to make that can't-be-refused offer. The manager will often take less than what the store originally paid just to get the products off his books. If it's *c*, you got the thrill of asking—and you've made another positive contact with a salesperson.

♦reasure Chest Trivia

Just how much do Americans spend in retail sales? According to the National Retail Federation, we spent roughly $2.5 trillion in 1997.

Sticker mania

What about the merchandise that's already got a sale sticker on it? You can negotiate for it too, so don't take that sticker as the final price. You can tell if the product has been on the shelf for a while, either by checking on it every time you come into the store or by the amount of dust that may have accumulated on its surface. When you find a likely candidate—an item that hasn't moved in weeks—bring it to the department manager and ask if he'll take less. You'll be surprised at how often the answer is yes. If it's no, ask if it might come down in price later. Even if the answer is still no, ask again the next time you come in (providing that you don't ask every day—your objective is not to drive them insane).

What *is* your objective? To remind the department manager that the merchandise in question is wasting space on the shelf and that he's got a willing buyer in you. Sooner or later, he'll probably give you a steal of a deal on it.

⬛ xpedition Tip

You don't have to wait until something's already on sale to start negotiating a sale price. If a fancy new product's just come in and is still expensive, ask when it's likely to come down. Pose your question in a polite, interested fashion and you should get an honest, thoughtful answer. Decide if it's something you can wait on or if you'd rather buy a cheaper, less snazzy model. If you decide to wait, you can keep checking back, building your rapport with the salesperson, until the time is right.

E xpedition Tip

When you find that a store's having a clearance sale, what you see on the mark-down tables is often just the tip of the iceberg. Check back every few days until the sale is over—you might discover new additions to that bevy of discounted goodies on each visit. Find out when the sale ends and check back at the end of the last day for the ultimate in mark-down bargaining.

The riches in the back room

If you could take a peek into a store's back room, you'd see all sorts of one-of-a-kind goodies tucked away, merchandise that's perfectly good, even brand-new, but can't be sold as new. Sometimes these items are displays—a television, refrigerator, or table that's been out on the floor for customers to view. They look sharp, have never been used, and may not even have been plugged in. But what happens when a newer model comes along or when that particular version goes out of stock?

The store has to get rid of the old model, even though there's absolutely nothing wrong with it. Because that model's been out in the public eye for several weeks or months, it can't be called new. The original packaging has usually long since disappeared, and the accompanying booklet (cautioning not to use electronics underwater and providing programming instructions) probably disappeared as well. But the savvy bargain hunter takes this as a challenge.

We bought a brand-new Whirlpool electric range for $150 that originally sold for $450. It wasn't in a box, but that was good—less cardboard to break down and throw away. It didn't come with the instruction booklet, but that was okay—we could figure out how to turn it on. We loaded it onto the back of our pick-up truck and drove away.

Once in our kitchen, we set it up, plugged it in, and proudly popped in a casserole. And listened to it beep—and beep and beep. Apparently it wanted something, but without any instructions, who knew? Well, we'd been through this type of thing before. We have a $200 cordless telephone/answering machine that we bought for $25. It works great, but it took us a month to figure out how to program the time. Until then, we never knew when people called. The machine would announce that the message had been taken on Wednesday at 3:10 in the morning when the actual time was Sunday at 4 in the afternoon.

Back to the oven. After we experimentally punched a few buttons, we discovered that all it wanted was for us to press "start." Programming the time was easy—all we had to do was hit the clock key, set the time, and select "clock" again. If you know how one set of electronic gizmos "thinks," you can generally figure out another.

If you're just not mechanically (or electronically) minded—one of those people who *still* hasn't figured out how to set the VCR even though you've got every piece of paper it came with—not to worry. The manufacturer will usually send you an instruction pamphlet. All you have to do is call and request it.

Expedition Tip

Don't panic if the TV remote has disappeared along with the packaging. You can get a universal remote for about $10 at any electronics retailer.

Manhandled by mechanics

Another goody in the back room's secret cache is the demo. This is usually some piece of electronic equipment (TV, boom box, computer) that's been out on the display floor, and because it's most likely been in operation for months, it can't be called new.

Some demos still have that fresh-out-of-the-box look. Others have obviously been well used—you'll see fingerprints that sometimes make them look like they've been manhandled by a gang of auto mechanics or numerous patches where various stickers have been applied and then peeled off in uneven strips.

Most people would never dream of purchasing a sullied piece of electronic equipment, reasoning that if it looks dirty it must be beat up—inside and out. On the contrary, these defects are usually only skin deep. A little cleaning solution, and that unattractive piece of equipment will sparkle like new and run great.

Today, electronics are designed to last, so a TV or CD player that's been up and running for a year is still a relative infant. And if it's been operating for that long, you can assume it doesn't have any bugs inside.

Computer demo crash course

A computer is a major purchase—one that's going to help you run your home or office, and possibly your life. Use the following tips to determine whether that darling demo is a deal or a dud.

Find out how long it's been a demo. This will give you an idea of how state-of-the-art it is—whether it has the latest bells and whistles or is already an antique. (If it's more than a year old, you may want to look elsewhere).

Examine it for possible flaws. Test the keyboard. Are there sticky or nonfunctioning keys? Do the monitor's contrast and bright dials work? You can sometimes negotiate a new keyboard.

Ask the store manager to get you past the demo loop into the system so you can test the programs. (Make sure they remove the lock-out that keeps the loop running before you leave the store with your new purchase).

Check that the other accessories—microphone, speakers, mouse, and cords—are present and accounted for.

Make sure you get the CD-ROMs for all pre-installed programs, including all the systems discs. Without them you can't restore your computer's applications if you have a problem. If the store's sales-people can't find the CDs, ask for an additional discount to make up for the programs you'll have to buy. (You can also call the manufacturer and have them send you a program package).

Ask for the full warranty.

That's it. Take that baby home and have fun with it. Remember, too: Don't get your feelings hurt if a brand-new upgraded model comes out a week later. You got a great deal because yours was being retired. And the newest model isn't always the best. Be happy with your proven all-star and let somebody else work the bugs out of the new one.

reasure Chest Trivia

Only 35 percent of all American households boasted a computer in 1997, according to the U.S. Energy Information Administration, but nearly 99 percent had at least one color TV, and more than 87 percent had a VCR to go with it.

In the eye of the beholder

It's not easy being a retailer. They often get stuck with mer-chandise that's been damaged in their own warehouses or on the delivery truck. Stock clerks have accidents with the forklift, or they load their trucks like Fibber McGee's closet—when it gets to the store and the doors are opened, everything comes crashing out onto the concrete. In clothing stores, customers who are a size 14 insist on trying a size 10 dress. The result? Instant ripped seam.

This is not a bad thing for the bargain hunter. Most buyers see beauty only in a flawless product. But to the bargain hunter, dam-aged goods are gorgeous—and another win/win situation for both you and the merchant. Most damage is not as bad as it may look at first glance. It might take less to repair than what you might think. Very often, the manufacturer will send replacement parts at no charge.

We bought a $300 GE dishwasher with a dented face panel for $225. It was the last one on the floor, the previous year's model, and it was damaged, so the department manager was more than happy to negotiate. We called the manufacturer and explained that we'd purchased a damaged product and would like a replacement. A week later, the UPS man delivered a new panel to our door. Total installa-tion time: five minutes. New look: perfect. Price: 25 percent off re-tail.

We also picked up a really snazzy $200 Hollywood-style oak medi-cine cabinet with tri-fold mirrored doors for $50. The only problem was that the mirrors were cracked. (*We* didn't do it so we weren't worried about bad luck). We carted the cabinet home in its opened box, propped it up in the hallway, and called the manufacturer. In a few days, the company sent us a new set of doors. Installation time: half hour. New look: stunning. Price: 75 percent off retail.

Enlisted as an ally

How do you nose out these terrific deals? Take a spin around the store. Chances are you'll see a refrigerator with a crunch on one side (forklift accident), an oven with a smashed door (fell out of the truck), or a washer with scratches along one side (shopping carts taking those corners too tight). Be a snoop shopper. Peer into every nook and cranny of the department you want. That damaged item will generally be tucked discreetly to one side—and you'll be surprised at how often the very thing you're looking for is just around the corner. Even if it's already got a sale tag on it, ask the department manager if he can do better. One of his jobs is to get rid of unsightly merchandise, so he might be delighted to enlist you as an ally.

Sometimes you find a damaged product that's been marked down, but it's still pricey. How do you get the manager to reduce the price still further? By explaining your options and asking for his help. Try something like this:

You: I'm interested in this dishwasher with the dented face plate, but it's awfully expensive considering it's been damaged. I can buy a brand-new, bottom-of-the-line model in perfect condition for less than this one here. Can you come down on it?

Department manager: Well, I could reduce it another $25.

You: I'd appreciate that, but that still makes it more expensive than this cheaper model. Can you at least match the bottom-of-the-line price?

Department manager: Hmm. I'd have to check the computer and see what our profit margin is on it (Checks computer). I could come down another $50.

You: Thank you!

reasure Chest Trivia

Furniture retailers have a higher profit margin—that is, they make more money—on upholstered furniture than on *case goods*, wooden pieces like tables and desks. Why? Case goods tend to get dinged up en route to the warehouse or the customer's home and the retailer has to pay to have them detailed and repaired. But nice, soft, upholstered pieces don't get damaged, hence they cost the retailer less money.

Damage assessment

As a bargain hunter, you've got to have a healthy imagination. Take a look at that damaged product and envision it made new. If it can't be magically restored, what can you do to hide or minimize its flaws? Lamps with torn or stained shades can be easily fixed. Buy a new shade or get creative and make one out of paper, wall covering, or fabric that you may already have at home. Wood furniture with scars or rings can be painted with whimsical scenes and colors—it's the current fashion craze. And if you can't make even a stick figure look realistic, use stencils. Ripped seams can be easily sewn. Do it yourself or take it to a seamstress—for the most part, their prices are often reasonable.

If that damaged item doesn't come with a warranty and it isn't working at all (meaning you have no clue what the problem could be), you're gambling. Often the store will cut the price to 10 percent of its value as an incentive for you to take it away. This is like buying a lottery ticket. The problem can be as simple as a blown fuse on a television, or as major as a compressor on a refrigerator, which has now become a storage cabinet—at least until you make a deal with a repairman to replace the part.

E xpedition Tip

Don't forget that every piece of damaged merchandise you rescue is one item that doesn't go to the landfill, which makes you environmentally aware and ecology-friendly.

Copier case in point

We found a lone desktop copier in the returns and odd lots section of our local warehouse superstore. It had been purchased by somebody, returned because it didn't work, sent out for repair by the store, and was now up for adoption. We kept our eyes on it for over a month but it didn't go anywhere, so we made the manager an offer which he promptly but politely refused.

We came back two weeks later and it was *still* sitting there, marked down further, but still quite alone in the world. So we made the manager another offer he could refuse. This time we pointed out that it didn't have its box, literature, or even a drum, which to replace would cost us $100 on top of the purchase price.

The manager decided we had a point and accepted our offer. We all agreed that if the copier didn't work when we got it home, we could bring it back.

Well, it didn't. But we didn't bring it back. Instead, we called the manufacturer, who cheerfully took our purchase information, gave us a three-year warranty, and offered to send out either a technician or a reconditioned machine. We opted for the machine. They shipped it immediately and it's been running happily in our office for over two years.

⎧E⎫xpedition Tip

Sometimes the only damage is to the packaging. Heavy, bulky items like assemble-it-yourself furniture, closet organizers, or weight sets frequently suffer packaging woes. If the cardboard's gotten wet or opened and re-taped a dozen times, it's liable to look pretty grim—and the store knows no one will pay full price for it, even though what's inside is right as rain. Often the store will price it at cost to get rid of it. If it's been around a long time or is the last one of a close-out, they'll reduce it even further. Peek inside and if you think it's okay, go for it, but try to obtain a guarantee that if it's missing parts you can bring it back. If you can't, make sure they reduce the price enough to make it worth your while.

Return to sender

You'd be astonished at the kinds of things people purchase and then take back to the store. We've seen major appliances that have been used—and in some cases used hard—and returned. From airless sprayers and hot tubs to small appliances, you name it and it's been brought back. Then there's that article of clothing with the seam ripped out (buyer heavier than anticipated) or with lipstick on the collar. It often seems customers purchase products as a sort of short-term rental, taking them back when they're finished with them.

Why does the store cheerfully refund their money? Often the merchant has a satisfaction-guaranteed policy, sometimes the management believes it's better to mollify a customer than lose him, or perhaps the customer is just pushy enough to get away with it.

All this is terrific for you, the bargain hunter. Sometimes there's nothing at all wrong with the merchandise, but it's marked down because it's been returned. Electronic equipment—from TVs and VCRs to CD players—frequently gets brought back because the customer insists it doesn't work. If you can buy it for the right price, it pays to take a chance and take it home. Often you'll discover that the only thing that doesn't work is the previous owners' mechanical aptitude. Either they didn't have it hooked up right or they couldn't figure out how to program it.

People will also return partially assembled build-it-yourself furniture because halfway through the project they discovered the simple instructions were beyond them. If you're not DIY-challenged you can pick these items up at store cost, bring them home and easily reassemble them.

Sometimes that returned item does need repair, but the problem is so minor that you can either easily fix it yourself or have a specialist do it for relative pennies. Several years ago, Terry bought a $65 pair of jeans at a trendy boutique for $9 because the zipper was broken. How could she resist? A trip to the seamstress cost $5 to have the zipper repaired. Today, those jeans are still going strong.

Tools for the serious treasure seeker

So you're planning to shop for those abused items and restore them to glory. Terrific! You're in for fun, the glow of accomplishment, and the pride that comes with doing-it-yourself .

Here's a handy checklist of the essential items that should be in every treasure-seeking bargain hunter's work space. (If you don't have them all, you can put them on your track-down list):

- **Hand tools:**
  - *Hammer*
  - *Screwdriver*
  - *Pliers*
  - *Channel locks*
  - *Adjustable or crescent wrench*
  - *Tin snips*
  - *Small carpenter's square*
  - *Set of wood chisels*
  - *Heavy-duty stapler*

- **Power tools:**
  - *Drill*
  - *Jig saw*
  - *Circular saw*
  - *Electric miter box*
  - *Hot glue gun*

Expedition Tip

Mend a weak leg on a table or chair by wrapping a piece of tin around it and then gluing it in place. The tin adds strength and can easily be bent to conform to odd shapes.

The last of its kind

We've discussed all sorts of goodies that you can find because they have some sort of flaw, whether real or perceived. But did you know that you can also negotiate great bargains on brand-new merchandise as well? Rob once bought a $3,400 leather sofa for $800 because the store was shutting down its furniture department. This is wonderful stuff that the retailer is no longer motivated to sell because they're never going to carry it again.

Retailers will sometimes advertise these kinds of bargains, along with the ever-popular going-out-of-business sale. But just because it's in the paper doesn't mean you can't negotiate a better deal.

Don't be fooled by stores that run perpetual going-out-of-business sales. This is your clue that they've grossly overpriced their merchandise so they can "mark it down" for unwary shoppers.

Pleasures of price-matching

They won't often tell you unless you ask, but many stores have a "beat the competition" policy. If you find the same item with a better price at another retailer, they'll not only match that price, but knock off 10 percent.

In our business (renovating beach properties), we're always running to the home improvement store for drywall, lumber, and other construction materials. And if you've ever done any building or remodeling, you know that these things don't come cheap.

Expedition Tip

Price-matching works for more products than drywall. You can use it to purchase builder's hardware, computer software, and

---

**B A R G A I N
H U N T E R ' S
J O U R N A L**

• In the right place •

Vernon Heywood of Laguna Hills, California, brought home a gorgeous Craftsman-style sofa from an upscale home furnishings store for 50 percent off retail. The only thing wrong with it was that the customer who ordered it custom-upholstered decided she didn't like the finished product once she saw it. So the store was stuck with it—plus quite a few more custom-ordered and rejected pieces as well. The store's solution: hold a liquidation sale.

Now, we have to admit that Vern was in the right place at the right time—he manages the store. But any bargain hunter can get the same sort of deal. All you have to do is walk into the shop: If there isn't a sale going on, ask if they have any returns. Then look them over and decide if you like them.

just about anything else. While you wait, the store will call its competitor to verify the price and that the product is the same. Then it will sell to you at the lower price. (Not all retailers will add the 10 percent discount, though). If you've already purchased a product and a week later you find an ad from a competitor who's selling the same item for less, head back with your receipt and copy of the ad to the store where you made your purchase. They'll generally refund the difference.

We make a practice of calling to check prices at a couple of different stores before we leave home. Frequently, you can come up a store offering merchandise at a dollar or so cheaper than another. We head for the more expensive store (which is usually the best one in town and the one where we do most of our business), tell them that their competitor down the road is selling drywall for less, and place our order. The savings add up quickly.

The store's not sorry we're doing this—in fact, they like it. Why? Because they know (and they're right) that while we're there, taking advantage of the savings on drywall, we're also loading up our shopping cart with all sorts of other materials. They're delighted that we're buying this stuff from them and not from their competitor. When you're looking to price-match, it's important to make sure both stores have exactly the same item.

Sometimes manufacturers will build in slight differences in the same products and give them different model numbers just to save store chains from having to price-match. For instance, a range built for one appliance retailer will have the little green or red "oven on" light on the right, while the same range designed for another giant appliance chain will have the light on the left. Possibly the knobs will be a different color. Different model number, different specs. No price-matching. But for the bargain hunter, this isn't always the case.

Keep in mind, however, that not all stores have a price-matching policy. If they don't, you can buy the item anyway or simply smile, thank them for considering your request, and walk away. Part of the fun of bargain hunting is the thrill of the chase, but it doesn't mean you're going to land every deal you go after. However, if you treat the store manager with respect and a sense of humor, he'll remember you the next time. And he just might come up with a bargain.

Expedition Tip

What happens when a slick new chain store opens in town? It offers lots of grand-opening discounts and its competitors gird themselves for battle—meaning they'll happily match those same prices so they don't lose your business to the new kid on the block.

The off-season shopper

Terrific bargains sometimes start with an on-sale price—merchandise that's marked down because its time is past, like Christmas trimmings in January. But not all sales come post-season, as stores often push pre-season goods to get shoppers in the mood to spend. There's a time and a season for every product under the sun, and as a savvy bargain hunter you should know what they are.

Follow along as we take a virtual spin through the retail sales year, alighting at each red-alert shopping event:

January. With the big holiday extravaganza behind them, stores are anxious to let go of the last of just about everything they brought in for the season, which means major mark-downs on all sorts of stuff. Look for sales on tools for Dad, sporting goods for Junior, holiday gift-boxed goodies like perfume and bath sets, chocolates, gourmet food baskets, and of course, clothing.

February. Home in on home furnishings and décor, including everyday dishes and dinnerware, because stores have a surplus of overstocks and returns on hand from the holidays. Add in the fact that this is the slowest month for this market and you've got a recipe for great deals. This is also a terrific time to shop for whatever lawn

BARGAIN HUNTER'S JOURNAL

• Oops! •

Now, lest you think we're perfect, and perfectly smug, know that we've had our share of misadventures. As just one example, there was the time we picked up a keen oak vanity cabinet that had just one flaw, a broken bottom drawer. Well, that didn't matter—we'd nail it shut and use the other three. Lifting it down from our truck bed onto the furniture cart, we got a little over-zealous. One of the remaining good drawers flew out of the vanity and onto the asphalt drive. Oops. Mangled corner. But we still had *two* good drawers! (Guess it's a good thing we don't work on loading docks).

A few weeks later we found another vanity that had been in an accident with a forklift. It had been nearly demolished, but the drawers were still good. We bought it for a whopping $10 and, sliding the drawers into the tracks of our other vanity, "made" the perfect cabinet.

and garden items are left from last season before retailers bring in new merchandise for spring. And before we leave February, don't forget to look out for Valentine's Day sales and for mark-downs afterwards.

◆ reasure Chest Trivia

Valentine's Day is truly heartfelt. According to the National Retail Federation, more than 36 million heart-shaped boxes of chocolate are sold each February 14th, with an estimated $1.1 billion in candy sales in 1999 and an estimated 900 million greeting cards sold and sentimentally delivered.

▣ xpedition Tip

While you can easily find boxes of Christmas cards after the holidays, stores clear out individual cards for lesser holidays like Valentine's Day, Mother's Day, and Easter immediately after the big event. If you want to stock up for next year, you'll have to move fast.

March. It's spring cleaning time for many major chains, which means aisles of marked-down merchandise to be replaced with new stock. Spring—along with fall—is also when new computer models arrive on the scene, so it's the perfect time to make a deal on those suddenly outmoded units that still work great. Hop into pre-holiday sales on Easter decorations. Get in the green with St. Patrick's Day sales, too.

April. Tune into sales on TVs and VCRs. Spring fever has consumers more interested in outdoor purchases than those meant for couch potatoes, so retailers are willing to deal. With winter over, now's the time to schuss into that set of skis you coveted all winter—along with other cold weather merchandise like snow mobiles, snow blowers, and space heaters. Don't forget after-Easter sales on decorations and candy. The trimmings will keep until the next year and the sweets will be just as sweet next month.

▣ xpedition Tip

You'll often find nifty deals on marked-down software at the computer or office supplies warehouse, and to make the deal even sweeter, the box comes with a big round sticker that promises a manufacturer's rebate of $10 to $20. Cool! But read the fine print before you get too excited—that offer may have already expired. (If it hasn't, make sure you send it in promptly).

May. Think Mother's Day and June brides and walk down the aisles with get-in-the-mood sales on small appliances, and fine china—the sorts of gifts retailers envision for the lady of the house. Then get in the swim with early-season sales on swimwear.

June. Summer gets into full swing, and as refrigerator doors across the country swing open over and over for cold drinks, compressors—the most expensive part of the machine—malfunction. Look for sales on refrigerators, as well as Father's Day sales on Dad-oriented merchandise like tools and ties.

July. Since the average shopper isn't thinking winterwear this month, it's a terrific time to snuggle up to great buys on fur coats. Conversely, it's also a great time to shop for swimwear as the retailer's summer season winds down and stores get nervous about how many bikinis they'll have left in stock.

Marks the Spot

If you live in or not far from a beach community, wait until September or October to shop for swimsuits and other summer clothing. Stores that stock—and mark way up—everything for the tourist know their market dries up once school starts so they routinely reduce things 50 to 75 percent.

BARGAIN HUNTER'S JOURNAL

• Chocoholic heaven •

Tooling around in Atlanta last March, we found ourselves in heaven, or more precisely, a fancy chocolate shop in a tony mall. We'd been looking for a souvenir gift of the city to bring home to friends on the beach, but all we seemed to find were coffee mugs and ashtrays featuring Rhett and Scarlett.

But here was a chocolate shop the likes of which are unheard of in our little beach town. We popped in to savor the scent and decided on the spot that our souvenir would be a box of chocolates. The salesgirl gave us free samples, helped us put together a custom box for ourselves, and then made a gift suggestion of an enormous five-pound Valentine box filled to the brim with luscious treats. It had originally been priced at $75, but nearly a month after the holiday, it was still unsold.

"And," the salesgirl assured us, "if you buy it, you'll be doing me a favor. I'd decided that if it hadn't sold by tomorrow, I'd buy it, and I don't need the calories."

We took it away for 75 percent less than its holiday cost and presented it to our friends—chocoholics like ourselves—who loved it. The only hard part was not eating it on the way home.

August. Go to the head of the class with pre-season sales on school supplies and end-of-season sales on water sport merchandise like surfboards, water skis, and scuba gear.

September. Fall into deals on trees and shrubs as nurseries and garden departments prep for winter and clear out the last of summer's greenery. It's more fun to plant in autumn when the air is mild than in the heat of July, and the fruits of your labor benefit from the whole winter before blooming again in spring. September's a terrific time to deal on plants and anything else lawn and garden (patio furniture, barbecue grills, and mowers) because retailers want to clear out their stock for winter. And don't forget summer coolers like air conditioners and ceiling fans that aren't in hot demand any more.

October. Write your own toy story with pre-holiday sales on kids' stuff. This is another season for silver and fine china deals as stores seek to unload the last of the summer wedding stash. Fall is also—along with spring—new computer model season, so get dealing on those just-replaced units.

November. Haunt stores for post-Halloween decorations as well as pre-Thanksgiving goodies. Because this month is the traditional kick-off for the holiday season, keep those bargain hunting antennae tuned for great deals among the hype.

Treasure Chest Trivia

The Friday following Thanksgiving, the day stores start the all-out blitz of holiday sales, is known by retailers as Black Friday.

December. Make a list and check it twice with deals on office supplies, which are not on most shoppers' lists this month. Just before and after Christmas, shop until you drop for next season's trimmings.

Treasure Chest Trivia

The four biggest confectionery holidays of the year, according to the National Retail Federation, are—largest first—Christmas/Chanukah, Easter/Passover, Halloween, and Valentine's Day, while the four biggest days for floral sales are Christmas/Chanukah, Mother's Day, Easter/Passover, and then Valentine's Day.

Next year's Christmas

Most people don't bother with Christmas in January because they're as worn out from the festivities as the stores are. Who has the energy to deal with still more mistletoed merriment? If you're a savvy bargain hunter, you do.

Start shopping for Christmas decorations around the 18th of December. Stores often start marking down holiday merchandise around then because—with less than a week to go until Santa puts in his appearance—they get antsy. They're worried that if their shelves aren't bare yet, they're not going to be. So if you need more stuff to fill out your décor, that's the time to start hunting.

But if you can—wait. It gets better. By December 26th, everything's down to 50 percent of what it was a couple of weeks earlier. And if you wait another week, prices can drop to 75 percent off.

CHAPTER TWO That's Bulk–
When Quantity
Buying Makes Sense

I t's not always a bright idea to buy a truckload of fresh milk or a shipping container of chocolates—the former will spoil before you can use it and the latter will tend to spoil you. But there are times when bulk purchasing is the way to go. In this chapter we seek out the secrets of buying big—not the warehouse club's Box O' Bagels, but major steals from regular retailers.

In the beginning: end lots

How would you like to redecorate the floors of your home with exquisite imported ceramic tile for less than the cost of serviceable old linoleum? Or install new designer carpet in any room for the price of a throw rug? Sound impossible? It's not if you're a savvy bargain hunter.

You'll accomplish these miracles with end lots. These are the home improvement retailer's version of refrigerator leftovers and you'll find them in carpet and tile outlets, wall covering centers, and of course, home improvement superstores. Instead of too many eggs, these stores get stuck with too much carpet, tile, or wallpaper.

This is frequently because of a miscalculation from somebody else's project. The contractor or the customer special-orders a particular product and discovers at the end of the job that they didn't need anywhere near what they first estimated. So instead of paying for it, they leave it for the store to dispose of. Sometimes customers will order an entire project's worth of tile or carpet and then never bother to pay for it or pick it up.

For the bargain hunter, both of these situations are like finding money. If you're willing to be flexible with your own home improvement ideas, you can redecorate for virtually pennies using elegant designer materials you might never otherwise dream of affording.

Gem hunting

How do you find these gems? The same way you locate all those other bargain hunter's jewels. Take a spin through the store. You'll usually find ceramic tile overruns or unclaimed special orders stacked on pallets near the back of the shop. Look for those first. The stuff that's glued up on display boards near the front of the store is good for getting ideas about what's new, what's hot and what going prices are, but it's geared toward the average consumer, not the wily bargain seeker. Occasionally end lots and overruns will be tagged with a discounted price, but often they're not marked at all.

When you find a pallet or stack of tiles that looks promising, approach the manager and inquire about the price. If the manager doesn't seem too amenable, help him decide. Remember that this is a friendly exchange. You want the manager to realize you're serious about your offer, but you definitely don't want to be belligerent. Some would-be bargainers get into trouble this way.

If a manager doesn't accept your offer, that's his choice. He knows more about his store and the management style of those above him than you. Make it a game. If he can play along you'll both have a ball. If not, you needn't buy at the set price.

Serendipity

Half the fun of this sort of bargain hunting is its sense of serendipity. You may go into a store looking for beige linoleum and come home with pink marble, terra cotta tile, or honey oak parquet. Naturally you don't want to buy something that won't match your décor, or something that is just unappealing, but use your imagination. It may not be what you had in mind to begin with, but if you can make it work, why not?

Sometimes the price is so incredible that you can afford to be a big spender and give somebody else a wonderful surprise. When Rob's parents bought a new apartment, we sent them boxes of $4-a-square-foot oak parquet that we'd picked up for 25 cents a square foot to redo their floors.

X Marks the Spot

Shipping heavy items cross-country can be prohibitively expensive—so buy them an airline ticket. We sent about 150 pounds of parquet from Florida to California for only $70 by sending it air cargo via Delta Airlines. The same overnight service through FedEx or UPS would have cost over $300.

Seeing the light

End lots don't have to be all about floor coverings. You may walk into the store intending to buy light bulbs and come across an entire tray of flashlights marked at 50 percent or more off. That's what happened to us a couple weeks before a recent Christmas. We picked up all of them and tucked them in with the shirts (75 percent off at an outlet center) we'd bought for the guys on our list. They were a big hit, an extra little surprise that said "thoughtful." After all, what male can resist a flashlight—or any other hardware store gizmo? When we found a bin of marked-down tool sets—pliers and screwdrivers in pre-packaged kits—we scooped them up, too. They made great last-minute gifts for unexpected guests.

Magic carpet

Carpet dealers nearly always have remnants—pieces of various lengths that are left over from somebody else's project. Carpet comes on huge rolls, anywhere from 90 to 180 yards in length. When customers buy a certain number of yards there's always something left over, and that's the remnant. Like ceramic tile, you can also sometimes find expensive designer carpet that's been special-ordered and then never claimed. These carpet dealer's woes can lead to terrific deals for the bargain hunter.

How do you know what to look for? Don't go to the samples glued up on boards at the front of the showroom. Those are for the consumer who wants to pay full price. Instead, nose around the back of the store. You'll see rolls of varying thickness, colors and styles propped against the walls or laid out on the floor. Those are the ones you should be interested in.

Make friends with the manager or store owner. Tell him what you're looking for. Ask a few questions about the remnants. Most people love to talk about their work and like nothing better than for somebody else to show a healthy interest in their world. This is how you develop a rapport—and a sales ally you can go back to again and again. While you're making conversation, ask these questions:

- *Is this a popular style?*
- *Do many people go for this unusual color?*
- *I see shag carpet is in again. Are you selling much of it?*
- *What would you recommend for a living room that's going to get a lot of wear and tear? (Or a guest bedroom that won't be used very often.)*

If your new buddy points you to a carpet that's way beyond what you're willing to spend, counter with, *That's out of my price range. How about this one over here?*

If that one's high as well, be honest: *That's more than what I wanted to spend. What else do you have?*

It's okay to let him know you're sniffing out a deal. You're not being cheap—you're buying smart. Instead of working against him, you're enlisting his help. This is the time when he'll show you the real deals, the pieces he probably wouldn't bring to the average shopper's attention.

Don't be square

End lots aren't just for carpet and vinyl. You'll find the same terrific deals on linoleum and vinyl tile, and for all the same reasons.

What do you look for? Once again, don't go to those glued-on sample squares first. For linoleum, seek out odd-sized rolls propped in corners or in special bargain bins.

For vinyl tile, find the boxes stacked on pallets at the back of the store or stuck out in the aisles. Then head for the manager and start negotiating.

When you buy odd boxes of ceramic or vinyl tile make sure each one has the same *run number,* which you'll find stamped on the box. They may all look the same and have the same name, but there can be significant variations in colors or shading. If you're not careful, you can end up with a floor that looks like a muddle of end lots.

What happens if that's all there is left? Three boxes of tile with three different run numbers won't look very good—unless you get creative. If you've got small areas such as bathrooms, foyers, or laundry rooms, you can use one box for each room and nobody (with the exception of yourself will possibly notice the difference. Or get creative when you lay out your floor. You can plan a "natural variation" in shades, a checkerboard or herringbone effect—or go even more eclectic.

A few years ago we purchased several hundred pounds of gorgeous pink-veined marble in Tijuana, Mexico, carted it 2,500 miles across the country to a beach condo we'd bought in South Carolina, and installed it six feet high behind the tub and along the walls—only to discover we didn't quite have enough to cover the floor. Solution: We laid the rest of our tile in a border around the room and placed carpet that matched the bedroom in the center. And it worked! It looked classy and was actually warmer under cold-morning feet than marble would have been.

Expedition Tip

Ceramic and vinyl tile often gets marked down because the style has been discontinued. If you or your installer makes a major goof on installation or if you gouge a hole in it next year, there's no going back for another box. Keep this in mind and consider buying an extra box to store for those unexpected accidents.

Presenting the package deal

The retailer will frequently give you an even better bargain if you take more than one end lot off his hands and make a package deal. You have to be willing to move quickly—before another bargain hunter comes along—and you have to think fast about *where* you can use an odd-sized lot, but you can come away with a terrific deal.

BARGAIN HUNTER'S JOURNAL

• Carpet ride •

We just carpeted our entire house in a top-of-the-line Berber for $175. We weren't looking for Berber—in fact we'd always claimed we weren't too crazy about it. But when we came upon 166 yards of the stuff originally priced at $1,900 and bargained it down to $175, we couldn't resist.

Why was it such a steal? One reason was that the rolll had been dragged across an entire warehouse floor or possibly even over an oil-slicked driveway, as the once-light oatmeal color was dirty and the carpet itself torn. Nobody in their right mind would want to buy it—except us. (We looked beneath the top layer of dirt and discovered that the rest of the roll was perfect).

Another reason was that the roll—which had been special-ordered and then never claimed—was 15 feet wide, and the display/cutting machine at the store can only handle 12-foot rolls. The carpet had been in the back room for nearly a year and had never seen the fluorescent light of day.

By the way, we decided we love Berber. It's in, it's classy, it feels good beneath bare feet, and every time we look at it we remember our great bargain.

Instead of buying only that perfect shade of rose for the bathroom floor, offer to take those boxes of Mexican pavers for the kitchen, and then possibly that stack of pickled oak parquet for the entry hall. By going the package deal route, you can redecorate three rooms of your home for less than the price of doing one at retail. If you hadn't planned on redoing every room in the house, but the deal's too good to pass up (and doesn't pinch your pocketbook), go for it anyway. You can store the extra materials in the garage until you've got time to do it yourself or until you negotiate with an installer.

Like end lots, package deals aren't just for flooring. The entire shopping world is full of possibilities. We discovered the joys of books on tape during our travels across country, and an audio books vendor at a swap meet in Southern California who carries just about every title you can imagine. Every year we see him, we select tapes that would sell for $14.95 and up retail, and then make him a deal.

E xpedition Tip

Always, always remember to thank the vendor or manager for giving you the deal. People like to be appreciated no matter what the situation is, and especially when they're essentially (by giving you a deal) also saving you money.

Tiny snowmen

Make sure you've got your creative-thinking cap on while you're bargain hunting. If you find something that's too terrific a deal to pass up but you're not sure what you'd do with a whole truckload full, come up with a new use for them.

One holiday season, we fell in love with a selection of snowpeople ornaments which, after Christmas, were marked at 75 percent off, and discovered that the store had a hundred of them in the back room that had never been put on the shelves. A great opportunity for an end lot deal, but what would we do with a hundred tiny snowmen and their mates? After we mulled it over, we decided they'd make wonderful tokens tucked in among the ribbons on gift wrappings.

Then we found 50 colorful cotton futon covers marked down from $60 to $10 each. Who has—or wants—50 futons? Not us. But we decided they'd make excellent mattress covers for our beach rentals and would be far less expensive than the traditional ones that go for $12.75 or more apiece. So off we went to the manager and offered to take the lot for $1 apiece. It worked—and now we've got 50 colorful "mattress covers."

▉xpedition Tip

Retailers often reward their sales associates with a monetary bonus for selling package deals—which means the salesman *wants* to work with you. If he can negotiate a sale where you buy not just the computer, but the printer, scanner, and extended warranty contract as well, he's in heaven. By bargaining your way to a great deal, you're helping him put extra money in his pocket, too!

▉xpedition Tip

When you find an end lot of a non-perishable product you or someone you know loves, go for the grand gesture—buy it all. There's nothing quite as much fun as watching the look on somebody's face when you present them with a major selection of their favorite things.

▉reasure Chest Trivia

People in the South spend more shopping dollars than those in any other U.S. region, according to the National Retail Federation. The second biggest spenders are Midwesterners, followed by residents in the West, while Northeasterners spend the least.

Buddy buying

Sometimes you just can't use 47 jars of fancy imported French preserves, but the deal you'll get if you buy them all is too great to pass up.

This is where you call your friends, tell them about your great bargain and invite them to participate. By the time you divvy up the goods between you and a pal or two, you've all got gourmet goodies for many mornings of fine dining, plus enough to give away as great hostess or holiday gifts.

In Rob's family, where they know great Mexican food, whoever makes the three-hour drive to Tijuana buys enough tortillas and *pan dulce* (sweet breads) to spread among several households. They're inexpensive when bought in-country, and they're *delicioso*. Somehow they never seem to last, even if you try hiding them in the freezer.

We once brought back 12 dozen flour and 5 dozen corn tortillas from Guerrero Negro, a small town on the Baja peninsula. And in two weeks there wasn't a single one left.

Expedition Tip

If you're an expatriate of another country or even another state, you know how you crave that certain something you just can't get in your new digs. If you've got family or friends from the same region, put together an informal buyers club whenever somebody travels back home and have them bring back enough for the crowd.

Vacation values

Rob's family are not only terrific organizers of authentic eats, they're also all-stars at putting together the perfect trip. They round up a dozen or more vacationers, then contact their travel agent and negotiate terrific prices on everything from air fares to condominium rentals.

The secret is in the numbers. Air and cruise lines will often provide discounts for tickets bought in bulk, which accounts for a good portion of savings. With everybody sharing the cost of lodging, they can all comfortably afford to stay in swanky accommodations. They've booked elegant hotel rooms in Bangkok and a villa in Puerto Vallarta with its own maid, cook, and terrace swimming pool—for reasonable prices!

Hold the phone

You don't have to travel to take advantage of buddy buying. You can phone home great savings on cellular phone costs by signing up with several friends or relatives. Cellular services are increasingly competitive, so the provider you choose will be delighted to count you and whoever you bring along as their customers instead of the competition's.

Shop around first and talk to people who use different services and different companies so you know which stand out from their competition. Wait until one of these companies offers a promotion giving you the latest in cellular technology—such as one of those cool phones that fit in a pocket—either for a small fee or free altogether. Head over to the sales store—often there are only a few in stock and when those are gone, so is the special promotion.

What do you say to get a great buddy deal? Try something like this:

You: I saw your ad for a free phone and I'd like to get one.

Salesperson: Good! All you have to do is sign our 25-cents-a-minute contract.

You: It's not going to be just myself. I've got four associates who want to go in with me.

Salesperson: Good! All they have to do is sign our 25-cents-a-minute contract.

You: That's five people. Can you work with us on your per-minute price?

Salesperson: Our price is already very competitive.

You: That's why we came to you.

Salesperson: I don't know. I'll have to check with my manager.

(She goes away and comes back with the manager.)

Manager: I understand you've got a party of five?

You: Yes. We're all business people in town and we'll be using the phones a lot.

Manager: I could probably arrange to give you a 20-cents-per-minute rate.

You: I'm not sure my people would go for that. How about 15 cents?

Manager: Well, since there are five of you, I can put you on our corporate rate plan that gives you 333 minutes for $50 and then every minute thereafter is 15 cents.

You: Good. Where do we sign?

BARGAIN HUNTER'S JOURNAL

• Filtering profits •

Don Hogan used to own a chain of tune-up shops and was always in the market for oil and air filters. A bargain hunter extraordinaire, Don discovered that often a filter manufacturer will decide to take over a particular market (such as all the discount or automotive centers in a region), swoop in, buy out the stores' entire stock of competitors' filters and put theirs in place instead.

What to do with all those oil and air filters? They certainly don't want them back on the market for consumers to buy. Don decided to make them a deal they couldn't refuse. He offered to buy each and every filter for 25 cents apiece and was gladly sold three tractor-trailer loads—which he resold to customers at his tune-up shops for $5 each. That's business bargain hunting!

Expedition Tip

Just because you get the phone for free doesn't necessarily mean you get off scot-free. You may still want to buy extra batteries, a quick charger, and a case, which can add up to $100 or more.

Bargaining for business

Most people know that they can pick up savings on office necessities like paper towels, paper for the copier, and economy-size tins of coffee by shopping at large members-only stores such as Sam's or Costco. But some businesses require particular kinds of products that you don't find at the warehouse center.

If you're a plumber, an electrician, an owner of rental properties, or an entrepreneur with a flea market, consignment or second-hand store, you can do yourself and your customers a favor by bargaining in bulk.

If you're a plumber, for instance, you can find kitchen or bathroom faucets that normally retail for $45 going for $6 to $20 at discount stores. When you do, buy them all. Even if you have to keep them in inventory for a while, it's worth it. It saves you money, and if you want to be a good guy or gal you can pass the savings on to your customers, who'll not only call on you again but also consider you a friend.

If you've got a home furnishings shop, you can pick up assemble-it-yourself furniture for 50 to 75 percent off when the manufacturer discontinues the line. All you have to do is cobble it together and sell it as is, or get creative and paint it.

Remember that part of your bargaining power is in buying all the store has in stock. When you offer to take everything, it makes an impression. The store is there to sell, and when they make a major sale to you, they're as happy as you are.

E xpedition Tip

What happens if you find a particular product on sale at a perfect price and you're set to buy out the store, but they only have two left in stock? Ask for a rain check. Some stores have a set policy in which they'll guarantee the sale price as soon as they get that item restocked, or they'll specially order it for you.

CHAPTER THREE Second Hand Rose

Some people love anything old, whether it's a 400-year-old antique or a four-year-old cast-off. For some, it's history that hooks them, the fact that a particular piece might have rubbed elbows with (or been rubbed by the elbows of) a Civil War belle, a turn-of-the-century beau or a Victorian duchess. For others, the magic is in the character of the piece—especially something that's well-worn and obviously been cherished—and the mystery of who once owned it and what their lives were like. For still others, it's the excitement of finding something not necessarily old but still functional and even fashionable, and gloriously inexpensive because it's second hand.

All this stuff is not only a bargain hunter's playground, but one of the hottest trends going. Barbra Streisand may have bemoaned second hand goods in the song "Second Hand Rose," but recycled merchandise is in these days. Turn to any decorating book, magazine, or TV show and you'll see room after room decked out in old furniture, fabrics, and accessories.

Entire stores are devoted to second hand clothing, toys, tools, and furnishings. And these aren't dreary Salvation Army way stations, but bright, cheerful trendy boutiques where you're as likely to see Mercedes and BMWs in the parking lot as rusty Pontiacs.

Why is wearing somebody else's old clothes or decorating with someone's used sofa suddenly so popular? One reason is that it's fun. The Baby Boomers who started their young-adult lives combing thrift shops for outlandish clothing with which to horrify their parents have come full circle and decided that everything old really is new again.

Another may be that Americans have ricocheted away from the old 80s mentality of gratuitous spending to focusing on home and family. Cocooning is in. People want to be surrounded by things that feel warm and cozy, and what better way to achieve that sensuous sensation than with things that have been around a long time? As we turn the corner of the new millenium, things might get a little scary. As a result, people want to wrap themselves in the blanket of a comfortable environment.

Previously-loved merchandise comes in many forms, from antiques with the elegant patina of age to garage sale cast-offs awaiting a new lease on life. In this chapter we explore how to sift the silver chalice from the tin cup and how to bargain with both the amateur salesperson and the professional auctioneer.

Treasure Chest Trivia

What's the difference between an antique and a collectible? It depends on who you ask, but generally speaking, an antique is anything more than 50 years old. (Some experts will tell you 75 or 100 years, so you be the judge.) A collectible, then, is anything younger than 50 or so.

That's garage, not garbage

Thanks to the old adage "one man's trash is another man's treasure," garage, yard, or tag sales can be fertile ground for the bargain hunter. What's the difference? There really isn't one, except for the minor differences of whether it's held in a garage (and on the driveway) or spread across a yard. And despite the fact that either of these can be called a tag sale, in many cases nothing's tagged at all. You have to ask. (Which is terrific, because the act of asking paves the way for bargaining.)

Whatever they choose to call them, people hold these sales for a variety of reasons and have various expectations about the financial outcome. Just as you do when you shop retail stores, you'll need to understand where the seller is coming from in order to negotiate the best deal. Some sales, such as moving and multi-family sales, usually advertise themselves as such, but you won't always know before you go.

Here's a rundown of the types of sales and the best bargaining techniques for each:

The moving sale. This one's an all-star event. When people start packing for a move, they realize just how much *stuff* they've accumulated and that they don't want to pack it all up and cart it to their new digs. Often they decide that their furniture won't fit in their new home for reasons of aesthetics or space. They might also decide (consciously or not) to start over fresh. Whatever the reason, they don't want to haul everything across town or across country. Solution: garage sale, where you'll find all sorts of high-quality stuff at terrific prices. Furthermore, because the seller's motivated to get rid of his possessions, he's very open to haggling. Bargain hunting rating: 5 stars.

Multifamily. This type of sale, in which a group of neighbors pitch in to share the setting up and staffing of the gig, is planned in advance. This means everybody's had time to consider what they're going to sell, dig it out of the attic, pry it out of the depths of Junior's closet, or unloose it from Dad's hands. Nobody wants to be the one with the least to contribute, so they all bring as much as they can. And nobody wants their neighbors to see their collection of microwave abused Tupperware, so they leave the really used stuff for the trash man. Thus, there's plenty to choose from and the quality is high. As another multi-family bonus, everybody's in a party mood, so they're ready to haggle and have fun. Bargain hunting rating: 5 stars.

Mini-estate sale. This is the one that's staged when an older relative goes to a nursing home or passes away, leaving behind belongings that no one in the family

BARGAIN HUNTER'S JOURNAL

• Know your pricing •

Leanne DuPay of Lake Forest, California, is the kind of bargain seeker others strive to emulate, the one who always manages to come away from the flea market or the garage sale with one-of-a-kind treasures for a fraction of their worth.

As a new homeowner in decorating mode, she found a vintage chandelier at a garage sale. When she inquired about the price, the seller informed her apologetically that it was really expensive—she was asking $50. But Leanne knows her stuff. "I'd been pricing chandeliers," she says, "and they were $900." Needless to say, she took it, with a smile.

Leanne bases a lot of her success on field knowledge. "You have to know your pricing," she advises. If you want to develop the same expertise, you can by shopping. "Spend lots of time just looking," our expert says. "Get a feel through mail order catalogs. Do a little bit of math."

Another of the secrets to Leanne's success is that she never goes on an expedition with just one item in mind. Instead she sets off with a mental list of five or so categories, for instance, vintage clothes, garden goodies, jewelry, and household

> page 57

wants. Some people call in estate specialists to handle the sale, but others just haul everything out to the garage or yard and host it themselves. You'll come across great finds such as antique furniture, dishes, and vintage clothing, but be prepared for products associated with getting older as well. Bargain hunting rating: 3 stars.

Cleaned house or garage. Could be nifty or not. Sometimes people get in a spring-cleaning frenzy and decide to sell everything. Otherwise, this type of garage sale is (for you anyway) an unsatisfactory alternative to the dump. Definitely check this one out but don't put it at the top of your list. Bargain hunting rating: 2 stars.

Sounds like fun. Here we have the kissing cousin to the house-cleaning variety. This type is usually not very good because it's arranged at the spur-of-the-moment and the seller doesn't really have anything to sell. Worth a drive-by but little more. Bargain hunting rating: 1 star.

Needs the money. This is about on a par with the spring cleaning sale. You might walk away with something wonderful. And you might come away with nothing. Bargain hunting rating: 2 stars.

The professional. You'll recognize this one because they're usually out there every weekend or so and their attitudes are more professional than the casual householder's. The deals you get won't be as good because the professional knows how to haggle, too, but you'll still do far better than if you went regular retail. Bargain hunting rating: 3 stars.

Marks the Spot

Make buddies with the professional garage salesperson. If you're looking for something in particular that he doesn't have, put him on the alert and have him hunt it down for you. He gets a potentially guaranteed sale and you get that lamp/table/sweater/tool you've been looking for.

The serendipity guide

How do you find garage sales? It's easy. One way is simply to let serendipity be your guide. Hop in the car on any sunny weekend morning and start cruising likely neighborhoods. You'll soon spot hand-lettered signs beckoning you to all sorts of enticing finds. Sales in middle-income neighborhoods are usually the best because people have enough money to have bought in the past and are willing to dispose of a lot of stuff. Lower income areas won't yield much because residents don't have much to part with, and really ritzy areas aren't so hot because people who have tons of money are often wary of strangers roaming their neighborhood.

You'll also often find great yard sales on country lanes—country people tend to be terrific collectors, and when they decide to clean house, they rely on a stream of Sunday drivers as their customers.

Another way is to check out the garage sales section in your local newspaper or shopper (those Thrifty Nickel/ Pennysaver throwaway publications that are all ads). It might seem silly to check the paper when you can find lots of sales simply by cruising, but these ads can alert you to sales in unfamiliar neighborhoods you might not have known about, usually contain descriptions of the type of wares that will be on view, and can even help you plan your route. (Our daily paper thoughtfully keys ads by neighborhood and provides a map to take along.)

Up with the sun

What's the best time to hit garage and yard sales? It depends on your goals—and your early-rising abilities. In some areas, garage sales start early—very early, often by 7 a.m. This means that the really rabid shoppers, including dealers scouting merchandise for antiques stores and flea markets, often show up even earlier.

If you want to get the best pick of all the goods on offer, you've got to grab that coffee cup and be out the door while the sun's still rising. On the other hand, sellers aren't particularly motivated to bargain

B A R G A I N H U N T E R ' S J O U R N A L

< page 55

items. Because she doesn't have her heart set on one particular object but instead leaves room for serendipity, she always comes home with something special. The magical usually presents itself, she says, when you're not looking for it.

On the other hand, Leanne advises, it's important to focus on your mental list rather than trying to broadside the entire flea market. Otherwise, everything becomes a blur and you go into sensory overload, looking at much and coming home with little.

What other secrets does she have up her vintage sweater sleeve? She doesn't suggest shopping a booth big on Fiestaware, hoping for some bargains on the trendy pottery—its prices will be too competitive and a deal unlikely. Instead, seek out the miscellaneous goodies the dealer's used to fill up his space. Because he really isn't interested in these side items and doesn't know their pricing, you can snap up great finds on the cheap.

while the dew's still on the grass. They've got a whole day ahead of them in which to sell their stuff. But since most people start garage-sale hunting early, the day starts winding down sometime after three in the afternoon. Customers dwindle. Sellers who have been up and at it since dawn get tired and are anxious to get rid of whatever's left. The prospect of dragging unsold wares back inside and putting them away is not appealing. When you show up at the last minute, that garage sale merchant is delighted to see you and in the mood to bargain.

The obvious problem with this technique is that if you wait until the eleventh hour, you run the risk of nothing left worth buying. What's a bargain hunter to do? Play it both ways. Start shopping early. If you see something you like but you think it's a bit pricey, ask the seller to come down. If you can't negotiate the price you want— and you're willing to run the risk of losing it—go on your merry way. You can always come back later in the day when the seller will be more motivated.

Here's what you say at eight in the morning:

You: How much do you want for this dresser?
Seller: $150.
You: Gee, that's more than I can spend. Would you take $100?
Seller (watching several other cars full of eager potential buyers pull up): No, we're pretty firm on $150.
You: What if I took the bed, too?
Seller: I'm afraid not.
You: Okay. Maybe I'll stop back later.
Seller: Sure. We'll be here.

And you toddle off to the next sale. You make it a point to return at four in the afternoon, the dead zone of the garage sale day, and to your delight, the dresser and bed are still sitting out on the drive-way, along with the seller, who perks up slightly at your arrival:

You: Hi. How'd the day go? It looks like you sold a lot of stuff.
Seller (who's kicked back, exhausted, in a lawn chair): Yeah, we did pretty good.
You: I'm still interested in the dresser. Could do a little better than $150?

Seller: I don't know, I'd have to ask my wife. (Calls her over from the garage where she's trying to figure out what to do with the things that didn't sell) Honey, what could we take for that old dresser?

Wife: Well, we had it marked at $150.

You: I could give you $90 if you threw in the matching bed.

Wife (looking at empty street): That was an expensive set when we bought it.

You: It's a nice set. But I'm buying it for my son's room and you know how kids are on furniture...

Wife: Well, I suppose we could take $100 for it.

Seller: We've got an old quilt that goes with it, too. We had it marked at $40, but we'd give you all three pieces for $125.

You: Thank you!

Garage sales finds

What kinds of things can you expect to find at garage sales? You never know for certain, and that's what makes them fun. Because garage sale sellers are more unsophisticated in terms of what they've got than an antiques shop or flea market entrepreneur, you can find terrific collectibles like art pottery, Depression glass, toys, and vintage lunch boxes (yes, they're very collectible!) for pennies.

Garage and yard sales are also great places to pick up vintage clothing (very trendy), linens such as quilts, comforter sets and towels, books, and furniture. You'll find tools, sewing, knitting, and crafts materials (all those enthusiastically started projects that never took wing), dishes, pictures, kitchen gizmos, costume jewelry, baby items such as walkers and strollers, and Christmas ornaments.

You'll also find a lot of junk—old plastic margarine tubs, books with titles like *Advanced Studies in Synthetic Chemical Modeling*, ancient computers and printers, anemic plastic flowers, and sheets that last looked fresh in 1957.

▄▄ xpedition Tip

Take plenty of cash. Garage sale sellers will usually take a check, but will be much happier—and thus much more willing to bargain—if you give them good old greenbacks. It not only relieves them of the fear that your check could bounce but also makes for a satisfying display when you pull out a wad of bills while in the middle of negotiating.

5 rules of thumb

Bargain hunting at garage sales can be a boon or a bust, depending on a variety of factors. Follow these five rules of thumb for finding the best driveway deals:

Season. Spring and summer are ideal yard sale seasons. The weather's balmy, the sun rises early, and people enjoy sitting outdoors interacting with passersby. But there's more to it than weather. By summer, people have come to the realization that all those wild, completely useless gadgets they got for Christmas are never going to be used, and they're ready to get rid of them. If you can pick up a $30 object priced at $10 for only $5, you can afford to take a chance that you'll never use it either.

As a final summer bonus, it gets hot and sticky sitting in the sun all day. By late afternoon, people are more than willing to give you a great deal just so they can get rid of things, close down and get out of the heat.

Although spring and summer are ideal, there is no bad yard sale season, so don't stop cruising when the weather turns cooler. You never, ever know when you'll find the deal of a lifetime!

Neighborhood. You'll find different goods in new neighborhoods filled with young families than in older ones where people have lived for years. If you're looking for baby items and toys, hit the new tracts. If it's vintage wares you want, try neighborhoods comprised of older homes first.

Seller's attachment. Most people you meet at garage sales are genuinely friendly and a lot of fun. But some curmudgeons are convinced that their well-worn cast-offs are worth an awful lot more than is reasonable, almost as if they don't actually want to sell them. If you bump up against one of these—and you can tell right away by their attitude—don't argue. Arguing isn't worth the effort because they won't change their minds anyway. Smile and move on.

Sophistication. Some people don't really know what they have—or don't care. To them the whole point of the exercise is to enjoy the sun, meet nice folks, get rid of stuff, and make a little money. Others, especially those few who hold garage sales as a part-time income opportunity, can tell cut crystal from pressed glass and are not about to let you buy the first for the price of the second. You can haggle, but be aware that it's going to present a bigger challenge than with the householder on a weekend selling spree.

Sense of humor. Most garage sale hosts are more than willing to admit that the throw pillows they're selling have seen better days—that's why they're selling them cheap. However, you can run into a select few people who can't take any criticism of their belongings. As a member of the bargain hunter's guild, you know not to insult a seller's wares, but those few humorless souls out there tend to take normal haggling as a blow to their pride. Again, smile and move on to the cheerful majority who are more pleasureable to deal with.

Expedition Tip

Bargaining for bigger stuff is the way to go, but don't get picky over pennies. Lots of garage sale goodies are marked at 50 cents and under. When you find these tidbits, take them for what they're worth and save your negotiating skills for the things that count.

White elephants and jumbles

Not all garage sales are found in garages. There's also the rummage sale, the white elephant sale, the jumble sale (a British term), the parking lot sale, and the storage space sale.

The rummage, white elephant, and jumble sales are all variations on a theme. As a fund-raiser for a church, PTA, or other nonprofit organizations, everybody contributes items that are sold in a hall or auditorium. Actually, the names seem in danger of becoming antiques themselves, which is too bad because they're delightfully descriptive: You *rummage* through a

**B A R G A I N
H U N T E R ' S
J O U R N A L**

• Picture perfect •

Rocky Akins is a busy restauranteur and realtor in Panama City Beach, Florida, who rarely has a moment away from one venture or the other. But several years ago, in his freewheeling bachelor days, his favorite weekend activity was to hop in his car and scout out yard sales.

One bright Saturday, after a morning filled with great finds, Rocky was ready to call it a day. He was turning toward home when he spotted one last yard sale sign, hand-lettered on a piece of cardboard, that pointed down an unpromising dirt road. Although he felt he'd had enough, the sign beckoned so he followed, finding a sale with nothing particularly interesting on offer except a Minolta camera in a plastic baggie. Rocky had needed a camera for a long time—it was a key item on his wish list. He asked the seller how much she wanted for it.

"Oh, it doesn't work," she said.

"Do you know what's wrong with it?" Rocky asked.

"No," she said, ready to call it a day herself. "Go ahead and take it."

What could he lose? Rocky snatched up the camera, thanked the woman and
> page 63

jumble of other people's *white elephants,* belongings that are useless to their owners but too good to throw away.

The parking lot sale is one that businesses stage to get rid of old inventory or furniture. Where we live, for instance, in an area with lots of small beachfront motels, you'll often find an impromptu sale of guest-worn dressers, headboards, bedspreads, and even beach-motif pictures.

While you probably wouldn't want any of it in your bedroom as-is, it's perfect to restore into something new, for furnishing a rental, or for setting up your daughter in her college apartment.

What about the storage space sale? People who've stashed their stuff in mini-warehouses sooner or later reach the point where they're sick of shuttling back and forth for belongings they once thought indispensable. So they hold a no-holds barred sale.

The bargain hunter's garage sale/flea market checklist

Make sure you're ready to roll with this nifty list:

- Comfortable shoes.
- Layered clothing.
- Sunscreen plus hat.
- Handy but tucked-away cash.
- Notebook for jotting down addresses.
- Swatches (paint chips, wallpaper/fabric samples).
- Window and/or room measurements.
- Tape measure.
- Magnet for testing metals (If it doesn't stick, the object is brass, silver, bronze, or gold. If it does, you're looking at a cheap base metal.)
- Cheat sheet with clothing sizes of relatives.
- Coffee or cold drink cup.
- Wet wipes for cleaning up after digging through old boxes.
- Tote or shopping bag(s) for carrying away treasures.

Expedition Tip

Not all garage sales take place on weekends. In some parts of the country, they're held on Fridays as well as Saturdays, and in some regions even on Thursdays.

Garage sale gem guidelines

When you discover those garage or yard sale gems that are electronic or mechanical marvels, it's important to ask whether it works. There's no point in carting home a prize you paid only pennies for if you discover it was sold cheap because it's doesn't work.

Tag sale sellers are usually wonderfully honest, but, of course, it's always prudent to ask the right questions, just as you would at the retail superstore. In some cases, all you have to do is graft on a new plug. It might be a bad fuse that's easily replaced or a corroded battery contact that can be sanded down. And remember that if an item isn't in working order, you've got real bargaining power.

So how do you know what might be a good bet and what's something best left for the trash man? Well, perhaps one of the simplest ways to determine if a piece of equipment is in good working order is to always ask to plug it in and try it out.

Keep in mind that TV sets can display a perfect picture for an hour or two and then go fuzzy. Obviously, you're not going to sit in someone's driveway and watch while the hours tick by, so if you've got doubts about the set use this as a negotiating tool.

If the product has accessories, make sure they're all present and accounted for. If they're not, you've got a bargaining chip.

Calling all fleas

In some parts of the country it's a flea market; in others, a swap meet. However it is labeled, this eclectic conglomeration of goods is a bargain seeker's ultimate mission, jam-packed with deals. It's also one of the few places in America where sellers expect to dicker. Many merchandisers have staked their claims through their knowledge of

BARGAIN HUNTER'S JOURNAL

< page 61

drove away with his new "purchase."

At home, he took the Minolta out of the baggie and turned it over in his hands. What could be wrong with it? Could it be something he could repair? "I opened up the battery compartment," Rocky recalls, "thinking that couldn't possibly be the problem, and peeked inside. The batteries were upside down and not touching the contacts."

He righted the batteries, and the camera worked perfectly. That evening, Rocky went out on a first date and brought his new camera along. He shot an entire roll of film of the lovely lady who shortly thereafter became his wife. It was love at first snap. Rocky and Zehra still enjoy both their first-date photos and the yard-sale camera that played a part in bringing them together.

bargain-hunting and spend their non-sales days tracking down end lots and package deals. You'll have to be sharp to turn the tables on them, but you'll also find it easier to do because there's no sales manager to appease and no corporate bottom line to contend with. Come along as we explore the tools of the flea marketer's trade.

Local color

If you've lived in your area for any length of time, chances are that you know where your local swap meet or flea market is held. People who live in larger cities and counties have access to a wide variety, some offering far better wares than others.If you're new to your locale (or if you suspect you don't know all the markets), the best way to find out is to ask—at local antiques shops, among your neighbors or co-workers, and even at the supermarket. You can also check the yellow pages and the newspaper.

Die-hard bargain hunters who have the time make a point of checking out flea markets wherever they happen to be. This is a fantastic way to soak up local color while seeking out new and exciting deals.

Flea markets are traditionally held on weekends—in some areas, every weekend of the year, in others once a month, and in still others only two to four times a year. You'd be hard-pressed to say that one season is better than another for the flea market trade, but (as with the garage or yard sale) your timing is the thing that will make the difference.

Marks the Spot

In some parts of the country, indoor emporiums run by a sole proprietor, brimming with junk and a few well-hidden collectibles, are also called flea markets. If you're willing to go through tables filled with junk, you just might happen onto a lucky find.

Flea market finds

What can you expect to find at the flea market or swap meet? Some venues, like the Rose Bowl in Pasadena, California, and Brimfield, in Brimfield, Massachusetts, are renowned for antiques and collectibles. Others are devoted to cars, guns and knives, even antique tractors and engines, but most offer an incredible variety of goods, old and new.

You'll see everything from brand-new clothing, cosmetics, tools and toys, and farmers market fruits and vegetables, to vitamins, houseplants, housewares, and tires. Then there are the vintage wares—furniture, dishes, toys, 45-rpm records, books, and blankets. If you can name it, you can probably find it.

Like the garage sale, you can find a fair share of junk too, but at swap meets the junk is more likely to be in the form of cheap toys, poor-quality clothing, and crafts projects like crocheted toilet-paper holder dolls. But sifting the chic from the chintzy is half the fun of the hunt, so get out there and get shopping!

Time travels

Take time into consideration on your flea market travels. Vendors start the day before dawn so they'll be set up when the show opens. As with garage sales, if you're among the first on the spot, you've got first pick of all the best stuff. The vendor won't be as inclined to haggle—he knows he's got a whole day of happy shoppers to sell to—but if you're willing to risk losing that ideal object, you can come back just before the market closes—close to four o'clock is good—and catch the vendor when he's tired and ready for home. That's the time to get the best deals.

Across a crowded flea market

All of the above brings us to a topic of considerable controversy among the flea market set. If you find that perfect item—tea cart, tea dress, or tea rose print—and it's a steal but still more than you planned to spend, do you buy it or pass it by?

Some experts recommend snapping it up on the spot. A flea market is not like a retail store where there are several of the same items in inventory or more can be ordered from the manufacturer. In most cases, it's a one-of-a-kind piece and a once-in-a-lifetime deal. So unless it's going to break your bank, they contend, you should buy it without hesitation. Others suggest you leave it behind, shop the rest of the market and then decide.

We say there is no one right answer. You can tell it's something that really speaks to you, as flea marketeers say, if you walk away and two aisles over it's still calling your name. Sometimes you'll know before you even leave the space. In that case, yes, buy it if you can. You won't be sorry.

If it's still speaking to you from across a crowded flea market, go back for it. Here's where you exercise your intuition, which gets better as you use it. If it seems that the dealer is getting a lot of action and that special item won't last long, hurry back and buy it. But if he seems to be having a slow day, you can shop the rest of the market and when you go back he'll hopefully be so delighted to see you he'll lower his price. You can guess wrong, of course, but that's part of the thrill of the chase. And when your intuition's right, it's even more thrilling.

You better shop around

Another thing that makes flea market shopping exciting is that the wonderful object you have to have is not the sole purview of one vendor. Because those swap marketeers often buy merchandise from wholesalers to resell to you, there can be more than one space with the same goods. So unless you're pretty sure it's a one-of-a-kind, shop around before plunking down your money—or you'll find the guy one aisle over is selling the same thing for less dough.

As a bit of contrary advice, don't count on the same dealer being at the flea market again next weekend with the same wares. Vendors, like gypsies of old, often travel from one show to another, so unless you ask, you can't be sure where you'll find them. Note that because their merchandise is eclectic and often one-of-a-kind, you can't be sure they'll have the same stuff next weekend either.

Stockpiling Melmac

One of the best things about shopping for pre-owned merchandise is the possibility that what you fall in love with today might be worth a lot more in a few years—that it will become a valuable collectible. While this is indeed possible, it's not a good idea to buy any item merely for its investment value, especially because the market is too unpredictable.

The general rule is that if you love an object and you can afford it, buy it. But if you're purchasing that Barney lunch pail or Teletubbies bath toy just because it may be worth hundreds of dollars somewhere down the line, put it back.

But what if you just can't resist the urge to stockpile and you want to start collecting something that will be worth a tidy sum in the next few decades? What should you choose?

"People tend to collect what they remember as a child between the ages of 7 and 14," says Jim Tucker of the Antiques and Collectibles Dealers Association in Huntersville, North Carolina. "Add to that hobbies such as golf and fishing, things that relate to their work, and family items such as china, glass, etc. For many years, glass has been one of the top collectibles and remains as such. Younger generations seem to use what they collect instead of putting it on a shelf, so they are buying dinner and glassware of the 60s and 70s."

And you thought all those Melmac plates with flowers and mushrooms on them were tacky!

Cool kitsch

How do you know what's cool, what's kitsch and what's just plain crummy? It all depends on you—your personal style, your imagination, crafting capabilities, and comfort level.

That's not tacky, it's trendy. If you're the type who can wear 50s pajamas in public and convince people it's the hottest trend in casual clothing, then the flea market is your personal playground. You'll have a ball with everything from bowling shirts to boxer shorts to those sequined cashmere sweaters Grandma wore that are now all the rage. But if you're more comfortable in jeans and t-shirts, don't buy the kitsch stuff. No matter how great a deal you get, if you can't feel good wearing it, it's not a good purchase. It'll only end up at the back of your closet.

Picture this. It takes a certain amount of imagination to shop flea markets. When you browse designer home furnishings stores, for instance, you see carefully designed sets displaying color-coordinated furniture and accessories. At the flea market or swap meet, everything's in a jumble—antique mahogany dressers next to black plastic futons beside bevies of baby togs waving in the breeze. Practice the art of separating that potential piece from the background and seeing it for itself. Envision it in your home or office, complemented by the furnishings you already have. Don't worry that it won't match perfectly—it doesn't have to. Eclectic is in these days. A mix of time periods is cool, so trust your instincts.

Make it so. If you can wield a needle and thread, a paint brush, hot glue gun, or hammer, you can turn trash into treasure. Vintage fabrics from chenille bedspreads to nifty 50s-print tablecloths can become skirts or jackets, curtains, or throw pillows. A nicked and scratched piece of wood furniture can get a new lease on life with a coat of paint—and you can add decorative touches like hand-painted or stenciled accents for the latest in designer furnishings. All it takes is a hot-glue gun to transform ratty picture frames into works of art, and a hammer, nails, and a shot of glue can remake that wobbly table into a sturdy dining table.

Take comfort in your own abilities. Many people have a fear of flea market flying. They think they don't have the ability to transform shabby into chic. All it takes is a little training, a little practice, and a little self-confidence. You can build all three.

Train yourself by browsing design and decorating books and magazines, watching decorating TV shows (turn to Home & Garden TV or Discovery Channel daytime for terrific tips), and window-shopping home furnishings at department specialty stores and boutiques. Take a spin through model homes, which are often packed with clever decorating ideas. Decide what you like, what you don't, and what works and why. For clothing rather than home furnishing fashion, follow the same game plan. Looking doesn't cost a dime!

Then practice. Buy a few items at garage sales and flea markets. If you go for low-priced goods, you can't make a major mistake. At worst, you'll have a good story and good fodder for your own garage sale (or for charity). As you go, you'll discover that you have a better eye for design than you thought you did.

Marks the Spot

Don't pass up old homes or buildings that are being razed or remodeled. You'll find architectural elements like fireplace surrounds and mantels, ornate carved woodwork from stairs and columns, stained or leaded glass windows, and ceramic tiles for the asking. You can also luck onto cabinets you can transplant directly into your own kitchen or bath, or use as extra storage space in the garage or laundry room. The best part? You can usually take all you can carry away as you remove it yourself. A word of caution, however: Never enter a worksite or take anything without permission from the owner or contractor.

Marks the Spot

Home builders offer potential buyers walk-throughs of exquisitely decorated models to show what their products can look like. But when the last house is sold, the model has to go, including all its furnishings and accessories, too. Find out when the model's scheduled to be dismantled and keep tabs, because you can often buy those pieces at terrific discounts. You win by taking home lovely items, and the design company wins because they don't have to arrange to haul away, store, and sell barely used goods.

CHAPTER FOUR Attack of the Antiques Lovers

O kay, we've covered those quintessential shopping adventures for the hunter of previously-loved merchandise, the garage sale, and the flea market. But that's not all there is. We've still got four terrific venues to explore: the auction, the antique shop, the estate sale, and the consignment shop.

Fair warning

People who are die-hard antiques and collectibles shoppers—and good ones—often avoid the auction because it's an unknown. They equate "auction" with the loftier houses like Sotheby's or Christie's and think you can only participate if you're a blueblood with millions to spend on a Van Gogh or Rembrandt. The truth, however, is that the socialite auction represents only a tiny fraction of the thousands that take place around the country every week—and a great portion of those are friendly, informal affairs that are held in country barns, tents and agriculture halls, and other eclectic meeting grounds.

Auctioneers take into account that their audience may be unfamiliar with the procedure and they explain as they go along. Not only is it their job to get people in the mood to buy and keep the atmosphere "up," they're also good hosts, entertaining the crowd with jokes amid the bid calling.

Miss Lula's home cooking

The country auction can be not only a great bargain site but a wonderful and absolutely free source of entertainment (providing of course that you don't buy anything.) One of our favorites takes place once a month or so on Friday evenings in a small farming community about an hour north of our home. For no more than a couple gallons of gas and less than a $10 bill, we get a lovely moonlit drive through the countryside, a ringside seat at one of the best (and perhaps the only) shows in town, and stellar home-cooked food.

The auction takes place in the county agricultural center—which bears a striking resemblance to a junior high auditorium—and the 25 or so potential buyers perch on metal folding chairs, around which are ringed the night's offerings. Off to one side, in the tiny kitchen, Miss Lula serves a selection of fantastic country cooking: home-made stew, meatloaf, and chicken-and-biscuits, followed by Red Velvet cake, lemon meringue pie, and apple pie—your choice of dinner and dessert for $3.75. Try duplicating that at any fast-food chain!

The highlight of the evening, of course, is the auction itself. It is conducted not by ultra-sophisticated gentlemen with British accents, but by a comfortable, middle-aged auctioneer in overalls with a deep Southern drawl. When his two assistants (who look like they couldn't hold a baby without dropping it) skillfully hawk delicate pieces of porcelain, it's entertainment in itself.

Wine and crystal

Much like a traveling circus, one of our favorite auctions comes to our town every three to six months. This one is ritzier but cheaper and just as much fun. It's held in the ballroom of a swanky resort hotel and features fine art, antiques, collectibles, and jewelry that the auction company brings up from various estates in South Florida.

Again, the room is ringed with goods, but everything else is different. The auctioneer and his half dozen assistants wear suits, potential buyers sit beneath a huge crystal chandelier, and instead of country cooking, we're treated to complimentary wines, soft drinks, and hors d'oeuvres. But admission is still absolutely free and you don't have to know anything more than how to have a good time.

▲reasure Chest Trivia

According to the National Auctioneers Association, auctions are one of the oldest ways on earth to buy and sell personal property. The earliest recorded auction was held in 500 B.C.

Tin tubs and tea towels

What can you expect to find at an auction? That depends on what type of auction you attend and where. Specialty auctions are held to sell automobiles, real estate, livestock, farm equipment, commercial and restaurant equipment, office supplies, manufacturers' inventory, and lots more. In fact, the manufacturer's auction is where flea market vendors often find their wares.

At country auctions, you'll find the same sorts of goods you might expect at a country flea market: pottery, Depression glass and porcelain figurines, pine, oak, and walnut furniture, and all those items so dear to the country collector's heart—old kitchen utensils and farm implements, stoneware, soda bottles, tin washtubs, and tea towels.

At fine arts auctions, you'll find bronzes, art glass, art pottery, teak and mahogany furniture, estate jewelry from diamond stick pins to diamond-encrusted Rolexes, Oriental rugs, and original paintings, lithographs, and prints.

That isn't all. Half the fun of auctions is in the mix of merchandise such as old and new, pristine and pretty banged up, originals, reproductions, and even cobbled-together retreads.

Fertile ground

So what makes the auction fertile ground for the bargain hunter? One reason is that it's one of the best places to find antiques and collectibles. People choose the auction as the means to sell their treasures because they have a better chance of selling them for a fair price. If they sell them at a garage sale, they'll realize just pennies on the dollar and if they take it to an antiques dealer they're likely to end up with only about 50 percent of an item's worth. (The dealer has to make a living too, so he has to buy cheap and mark up high enough to be profitable.) The auction's a good choice because buyers tend to get excited, inciting each other on to higher bids, where the price can rise significantly.

Okay, we hear you saying, if the price goes *up* at an auction, what makes it valuable for the bargain hunter? For one thing, not a lot of people attend smaller auctions—in fact, frequently a piece will go up on the auction block and come back down again without a taker. You might be the only bidder on something terrific, which means the price you set is the selling price.

Expedition Tip

Some items or *lots* (a group of objects belonging to a particular seller) carry a *reserve*. This is the minimum price the seller is willing to take. Even if you're the only bidder, you'll have to at least meet the reserve or the piece comes off the block unsold. There's also the *minimum bid*, which is the lowest acceptable amount at which bidding can start. This prevents you—or your competition—from smart-aleck techniques like starting the bidding on a Tiffany lamp worth $2,000 at, say $10. Don't worry about not knowing what the minimum bid is. The auctioneer will tell you.

There are regional tastes in auction objects as well as in fast food, so if you're savvy enough to spot something nobody in the audience is interested in, it's yours for the asking.

We used to attend a weekly auction in Charleston, South Carolina, for instance, where rusty tin washtubs were all the rage. The bidding for these things, mostly among middle-class, middle-aged ladies, was fierce. But lovely silver tea services went begging, with the auctioneer removing them from the action unbid upon.

Sunday drive

How do you find auctions? Check the classified ad section of your local newspaper. Auction ads not only provide a nice selection of current and upcoming events, but also list the types of wares on offer so you can decide whether that Sunday drive will be worth the trip.

Once you get used to attending auctions you'll become familiar with the auctioneers in your area. Each has his or her own style: the types and condition of merchandise they take on, the kind of crowds they attract, and what sort of minimum pricing they set.

When you see their names in the advertisements, you'll have a pretty good idea of what to expect before you ever arrive (or even *if* you want to arrive).

You can also find auctioneers and auction houses listed in the yellow pages. Call and find out when and where their next events will be held. You can ask to be put on their mailing lists, although once you purchase a few items at auction, the houses that have lists will automatically include you in mailings for upcoming functions.

Marks the Spot

If you have a computer, you can look for auctions near you (or near a locale you'll be visiting) on the National Auctioneer's Association Web site at www.auctioneers.org.

Secrets for auction success

Capture those bargains and bid like a pro with our secrets for auction success:

Check out the coming attractions. Most auctions feature previews, in which everything for sale is placed on display well before the main attraction begins, usually an hour or two before the bidding starts. This is done just so that you, the buyer, can check out any items that catch your interest. You can pick them up and examine them as carefully as you like. Remember: The auction, like its cousins the yard sale and flea market, is a case of let the buyer beware—once you've bought it, it's yours. You can't return it later like you can in retail outlets. It's up to you to give goods the once over.

Premium or unleaded. Find out if the auction has a buyer's premium, a percentage (usually 10 percent, though sometimes 15 percent) of the sale price that's added onto your final bill. If so, take the premium into consideration—that, including the tax, can increase a terrific bargain price considerably if you've purchased a high-ticket item.

Be an eager beaver. Auctioneers usually put some of the best stuff up for bid first to get the crowd interested and excited. But people are often hesitant to start bidding—they're insecure of their abilities or waiting for someone else to set the pace. If you arrive early and you're an eager beaver, ready to jump into the action, you can end up with some steals.

Expedition Tip

By arriving early and carefully shopping the previews, you can make buddies with the auctioneer or his bid assistants. Since not everything at auction comes up for bid, you can ask your new friends to make sure the piece you want goes onstage.

Be a late owl, too. By the time an auction begins to wind down, everybody's tired. Many buyers have already called it a day, while those who remain are likely to be overwhelmed, mentally trying to figure out how much they spent and why. If you can stay alert, you can latch onto great deals because the competition's pooped out.

Pray for rain. If the weather's bad, the turnout will be too. Again, if you're an on-the-spot bargain hunter, you'll have an opportunity for some steals because the other bidders are at home watching TV.

Don't drink and bid. It feels so elegant to sit back and sip that fine wine while the bidding rolls along, but don't overindulge. If you get into the spirits of the evening too much, you're liable to overbid. Keep your intake moderate or stick to the sparkling water.

Chill out. Half the fun of the auction is when the bidding starts going fast and furious. The audience gets excited and bids go higher and higher. This is, as Martha Stewart would say, a good thing for the auctioneer and the seller—but not for you. Decide during the preview phase, or when the item comes up for bid, what your limit will be and don't go over that amount.

Keep an eye on the pros. As you get used to auctions, you'll be able to spot the antiques dealers, just as you can at garage sales and flea markets. Watch them. It's a terrific way to learn what's worth buying and what isn't, as well as what are reasonable prices for those must-have pieces. The dealer, remember, isn't going to pay full retail because he has to mark up the price once he gets it to his shop. Being a savvy bargain hunter, you don't want to pay retail either, so you can learn when to stop your bidding.

Don't be shy. At larger functions, sit up close enough to the stage so the auctioneer or his bid assistants can see you.

Slow it up. If the bidding's going too fast on a piece you want, you can sometimes slow it up enough to think out your strategy. One way is to establish eye contact with the auctioneer—let him know you're about to bid but are considering the amount. The other way is to change the bid increments. If bidding is going from $100 to $200 to $300, for instance, try making your next bid $350 instead of $400. It throws off your competition and lowers the size of the bid.

E xpedition Tip

A few auction houses will arrange delivery, but it's usually your responsibility to take your purchase away with you. So if you're buying furniture, either borrow your brother-in-law's pickup truck or plan on driving home with table legs poking you in the back.

◆ reasure Chest Trivia

Sometimes you'll hear the auctioneer exhorting the porters—the lads responsible for carrying items off and onstage—to "Mix it up!" This means he feels he's losing the audience and wants to vary the mix of merchandise: a vase followed by a writing desk followed by a bronze ornament, for example, instead of a slew of furniture pieces all in a row.

Selling the estate

Estate sales are sort of a cross between the yard sale and the auction. They're generally held when someone passes away and the family decides to sell the belongings instead of divvying them up amongst themselves or giving them to charity. Estate sales are also held when a family moves and decides to start over fresh instead of lugging everything across the country.

Although these events can be held at an auction house, they're almost always held at the deceased's home. The action—like those murder mystery plays in which you're plopped into the thick of things—takes place in every room of the house and in the front and back yards. If you've got an inordinate curiosity about other people's homes, the estate sale is ideal for you because it marries bargain hunting with peeking into someone's nooks and crannies.

When Ol' Blue Eyes was young

What can you expect to find at an estate sale? Lots of vintage treasures but not much that's new or late-model. You can find

B A R G A I N
H U N T E R ' S
J O U R N A L

• The price of silver •

We were on our way to the home improvement store one gorgeous Saturday morning when an estate sale sign caught our attention. The day was fine, the neighborhood was upscale, and we sensed a deal, so we followed a series of winding lanes along the bayou until we reached the two-story home where the sale was being held.

We walked inside. The décor was high-tech and trendy—for 1959—and had apparently never been changed since. (A look, by the way, that's experiencing a big-time revival.) We skipped from room to room, but since we're not really into the Danish modern, formica-and-chrome look, we didn't find anything that reached out and grabbed us, except a boxed set of silver-plated flatware.

Most of the pieces were accounted for (which is often unusual), the set was in excellent condition, and the pattern was attractive, but the price of $250 was not. We took it to the estate sales rep, who said he couldn't lower the price because the sale had only been in progress for half a day and suggested we come back in the afternoon. When we returned around

> page 79

Frank Sinatra albums in the living room, bottles of Avon perfume in fragrances last made in the 50s in the bathroom, and sewing patterns and fabrics for some long-forgotten sock hop or square dance in the spare bedroom. However, unless it's an estate moving sale (and these are rare), don't look for Cranberries CDs or miniskirts in the bedroom because these aren't the sort of things older people buy.

You'll also find old and antique furniture, tools, lawn mowers in the shed, old magazines, Christmas ornaments, and books in the garage. Of course, there are also kitchen utensils, small and large appliances, silverware, Tupperware, fine collectibles, vintage clothing, and linens. In fact, you can even buy the potted geraniums and ferns.

◤ reasure Chest Trivia

What's inexpensive today that will be highly collectible in 40 to 50 years? "Probably everything," says Milton Talbert, Jr., of the National Association of Dealers in Antiques Inc., "if it is well preserved and still in its original package." Two specific categories of interest, Milton advises, are the State Series Quarters being issued by the Federal Mint in the year 2000, which recognize each of the 50 states, and any Y2K memorabilia.

Holding court beside the azalea bush

You'll find estate sales the same way you find auctions—by checking the classified sections of local newspapers and perusing the yellow pages. If you can't find listings under "estate sales," try looking for auctioneers or auction houses. You'll also find estate sales as you make your yard sale rounds—the professionals who run these events take care to post directional signs at frequent intervals.

Some estate sales are run like tag sales. You wander around and when you find something you like, you bring it to the sale's representative's attention and start negotiating a price. Other sales are run like regular auctions, with buyers standing around in the backyard and the auctioneer holding court beside the azalea bush.

Bargaining at estate sales is very much like bargaining at any other previously-loved merchandise outlet. You take the weather, the turnout, the time of day, and the general interest level of the participants into consideration, and start your negotiations.

◆ reasure Chest Trivia

Careful! In America, *silver plate* means a coating of silver electroplated onto a base metal and is not as fine or expensive as sterling silver. But in England, *plate* means sterling. So if you happen to be in Britain or you're dealing with British goods, don't pass up the plate as second class.

✖ Marks the Spot

Used furniture stores are wonderful places to shop for antique and closeout furniture. The selections—everything from swanky 30s liquor cabinets and clunky 1946 metal office desks to red brocade couches that look like they came from a bordello—are so funky that just window-shopping is fun.

Raiders of the lost consignment

If you're into previously-loved merchandise, yet another delightful avenue for bargain adventuring is the consignment store. This is a shop that, instead of purchasing an inventory of merchandise, accepts items from private parties and displays them for resale. When a piece sells, the store then splits the profits with the owner. So here again, you have the opportunity to purchase one-of-a-kind valuables you'd be hard pressed to find down at the mall or Wal-Mart.

But it gets better. The thing that makes consignment shopping a mecca for the bargain hunter is that at most stores,

four, he said he still couldn't lower the price because the sale had another day to run.

"We already came back once," Rob said pleasantly. "I don't want to have to come back again. Can you work with me on this?"

The rep glanced around the room, where there wasn't much activity. He checked a column of figures on the table and looked at the box of flatware. "I could let you have it for $200."

"That's kind of steep," Rob countered. "It's missing several dinner forks and a knife, It's also not a popular pattern." The rep gave another weary sigh. "How about $175?"

"We'd take it for $150," Rob said.

"Done." The rep wrote up the sale, then started taking the silver out of the box.

Rob stopped him. "We need the box, too."

"Oh, I can't do that," the rep said. "That was just for display." When Rob subtly withdrew his credit card, the fellow relented. "I can let you have it for $40."

"Make it $20," Rob said, "and it's a deal."

We took the silver and the box, and left happily. Lest you think we left behind a miserable sales rep, he was smiling too.

merchandise gets marked down on a regular basis. Some go on a schedule of about 20 percent for every three weeks an item sits in the store. Others leave objects at a set price for the first 30 days they're in inventory, then mark them down 10 percent a week. If you spot a beauty of a butler's tray, for example, at a 20-percent plan, and it's priced at $150, you can wait. In three weeks or less (depending on how long it's already been in the store), it'll cost $120. Three weeks after that the price will only be $96. Then it'll go down to $76.80.

How do you know when that great piece first came into the shop? The date will be marked on the sale tag or sticker. You can add the thrill of gambling to all this because you never know whether the piece will remain in the store while you wait for the price to go down or if someone else will come in and snap it up.

Here's another consideration: If a piece goes down to 50 percent of its original price and still doesn't sell, it doesn't get marked down again. Instead the owner is called and asked to come pick the item up. Or it gets donated to charity. If you hesitate too long, you lose.

◆ reasure Chest Trivia

Why do consignment shops mark things down with such regularity? To move inventory. Unlike a retail store that stacks 10 pairs of the same jeans on the shelf or has a half dozen of the exact same table in the warehouse, the consignment store depends on quick turnover to keep customers coming back.

Furs to furniture

What can you expect to find at the consignment store? It all depends on what type of shop you're visiting. You'll see everything from bridal gowns to maternity clothes, furs to furniture, baby togs, toys, computers, home accents, sporting goods, men's wear, and more. Although many stores mix and match these categories, most of them stock furniture and family apparel.

Consignment furniture shops can play host to such diverse items as a 200-year-old sideboard, a nifty 50s coffee table, and a two-year young sofa. You'll also find both antique and modern pictures and prints, Chinese cloisonné vases, silver tea sets, and lamps galore. Half the fun is that you never know from one day to the next what you'll discover when you walk in the door.

Consignment clothing shops tend to fall into two camps: the designer duds boutique featuring name-brand garments for resale, from names like Donna Karan, Anne Klein, and Oscar de la Renta, and the happy-go-lucky shop where cotton rompers nestle on a rack next to last season's jeans.

You'll also find hats, shoes, belts, and jewelry in among the clothing, and it's not at all unusual to find a designer dress with the price tags still attached at a steal of a price. Consignment storeowners normally mark goods at about one-third to one-fourth of the original retail price—or less—depending on desirability and condition.

reasure Chest Trivia

Recycled merchandise really is in! According to the National Association of Resale and Thrift Shops, resale is one of the fastest growing segments of the retail industry, with more than 15,000 shops across the country.

The second time around

Where do you find consignment stores? Not at the mall, because the rent's too high, and not generally in the trendiest part of town for the same reason. Most consignment stores are tucked away in small strip centers, but we've sometimes seen them in ritzy office areas and storefronts, cheek-to-cheek with upscale boutiques. Like the mercurial merchandise within, you never know where a consignment emporium might pop up.

The more affluent the neighborhood, the better the goods. You'll find fantastic, barely worn designer togs in tony areas, because people can afford to buy the garments in the first place and trade them for something new after they've been worn to a single party. People who live in poorer areas, on the other hand, buy their clothes at Walmart or Kmart and can't afford to part with them until they're ready for the rag bag.

If you're not into a $2,000 party dress or tux for $200, it still pays to look for consignment shops in upscale suburbs. You'll find terrific kid's clothes as well as plenty of fabulous "regular" stuff for the whole family at rock-bottom prices. (Four-dollar jeans are not uncommon and neither are $5 shirts).

The same rule holds true for furniture, toys, tools, and sporting goods. People in higher income areas yield better consignments than those on the other side of the tracks. Keep your eyes open for consignment stores as you toddle around town. Don't be afraid to try them out. Recycling is hot these days. Eco-buying is in. To paraphrase the old Frank Sinatra song, merchandise is lovelier the second time around.

Expedition Tip

Old is often better. You can buy a really great solid wood piece of furniture at a consignment store for about the same price you'd pay for something similar made of particle board at a home furnishings store.

Emporiums of gently used goods

If a consignment shop is a recycled merchandise outlet and so are a thrift shop and a resale store, what's the difference? Though they're all emporiums of gently used goods, and thus all resale stores, a thrift shop is run by a nonprofit organization such as Goodwill, a children's hospital charity, or a church group. These stores usually get their merchandise through donations, but they can also operate on a consignment basis.

Resale stores get their goods by purchasing them outright from private parties, while consignment stores, as you know, consign their inventory—which typically comes from individual owners but can also come from wholesalers.

Treasure Chest Trivia

In case you thought the Goodwill store was all musty dark corners that nobody ever actually goes into, think again. Goodwill's retail sales of donated goods in 1998 came in at $788 million.

X Marks the Spot

The offerings at Goodwill stores are not all hand-me-downs. Goodwill also purveys brand-new goods (mostly overstocks and irregulars) from name retailers including Target, JC Penney and Natural Wonders under a special Surplus Merchandise Program.

The formula of five

Now you know all about the great deals to be found at consignment stores. But how do you determine whether to snap up that piece while it's a great deal or wait until it's a fabulous one? Follow these five formulas to get steals on consignment goods:

Check the interest. Ask if there's been much interest in the item. If it's caught your attention and no one else's, you can feel safer playing the waiting game. But if lots of folks are making eyes at it, you might want to grab it while you can.

History lesson. Ask if the store has stocked similar items in the past, how long ago, how fast they went, and what they ultimately sold for.

Hello central. If an item has been in the store for a while, ask the shopkeeper to call the consignor and find out if she'll take a price lower than what it's currently marked at. This strategy often works. Some consignors have already told the store they'll take a certain percentage off. Others, particularly if the object has been on the floor for several weeks (especially if it's heavy furniture), would rather sell it cheap than have to come pick it up.

Take your pulse. Get a reading on your emotional pulse in the matter. How badly do you want the item? If it really speaks to you and you can afford to shell out the beans, do so before it's gone. If, on the other hand, you can sail out the door with nothing more on your mind than the root beer float at the ice cream parlor next door, then wait and see what happens.

Trust yourself. Go with your instincts. The more bargain hunting you do, the better you'll get.

BARGAIN HUNTER'S JOURNAL

• Go for it! •

Terry's sister's pal Leanne DuPay (a serious Second Hand Rose bargain hunter) has uncovered some wonderful finds in some really dismal places. Exploring a "hideous" thrift shop—the kind where you have to wash up after a good prowl through the merchandise—she and her husband came across a decanter celebrating the first 100 years of baseball for $6. With a home sports bar, they decided this was a find worth the price. On a subsequent trip to Chicago, they found a duplicate decanter, kept delicately in a glass case, priced at $65.

How do you go after the same kind of bargain big game? "You have to be willing to get your hands dirty," Leanne says. When you find that great deal, be ready to fire. "If you love it and you can afford it, go for it," the Lake Forest, California, resident advises. "Sometimes you know it's awesome and you think 'Boy, did I luck out!'"

Expedition Tip

Take advantage of Bargain Seeker's Secret No. 4 and make buddies with the consignment store staff. Sign up for their mailing list—you'll get sale notices, customer-only premiums, and other tips on what's on the top of their resale stack.

Clothing caveats

When you shop consignment or other resale clothing outlets, you sometimes feel like you've hit a bargain bonanza. Everything is so inexpensive it's hard not to buy up the whole place. But the savvy bargain seeker shops wisely and doesn't get carried away buying simply for the sake of a sale price. Keep these caveats in mind:

The match test. Consider whether the piece of clothing you found will match the other clothes in your closet. If not, it may not be such a hot deal.

Dry cleaning decisions. Look at the label. If it's something you'll wear often and it requires dry cleaning, you may end up spending more on cleaning bills than you will on the garment itself. (Some "dry clean" items can be gently or machine laundered, but you don't know until you try, so be careful.)

Irregular inspection. Some garments end up at the resale store because they're manufacturer's irregulars, meaning the cloth from which they were cut had a run or other textile flaw, they were cut on the bias (which means they twist instead of laying flat), they're torn, stained, or the seams are crooked. In some cases these flaws are minor or can be easily disguised. In others, they ruin the garment. But you can get so excited about your find that your eye skips right over a major goof. Take a careful look before you get to the cash register and again when you place your find on the counter—that's when you spot the flaw. If you ask, the salesperson will help you check over your finds.

Run a size check. Shoppers don't always put things back in the right size section of clothes racks. Try checking a size or two up or down from your own for garments that should be in your sector.

Expedition Tip

In all pre-owned merchandise venues, be it garage sale, thrift shop, flea market, or consignment store, you'll find dusty boxes tucked into corners—things that have come in for inventory but haven't been unpacked. Be the first to investigate. The grungier the box looks, the less interested anyone else is liable to be, and often, the better the discovery. Plus, if your find hasn't been tagged yet, you can frequently set your own price.

Antiques alley

The antiques shop is a haven of pre-loved merchandise, a store that's by definition a resale extravaganza. You can find antiques dealers in every city and town, and in tiny hamlets out in the country. Some shops feature only fine antiques—high-priced objects bearing the patina of centuries of care. Others handle collectibles, bits and pieces of glass and brass, lunchboxes, hat boxes, cigar boxes, old postcards, old cookbooks, and well-used kitchen utensils. Still others specialize in garden gems or architectural artifacts.

Everything old

Whatever the goods, just because it's called an antiques store doesn't mean everything in it is old. Many antiques dealers sell reproductions, furniture that is crafted with care and of far better materials than the particle-board stuff you assemble yourself. Reputable shops will mark the item as a reproduction right on the tag so there's no misunderstanding. Others take the attitude that if you don't ask, you don't need to know.

But it's not that simple. In the world of fine antiques, you can find brand-new reproductions and old, or even antique, reproductions. In other words, you might find a 50-year-old highboy that's a reproduction of an 18th-century Chippendale. It's old but it's not an original.

B A R G A I N H U N T E R ' S J O U R N A L

• The bookcase •

As professional writers and inveterate readers, we're always accumulating books, yet we never have enough places to stash them. When we happened on a beautiful fruitwood bookcase at a favorite consignment store in California, we were hooked. An antique reproduction, it was six feet tall and four feet wide, with a carved shell pediment, 10 shelves, and two sets of double doors inset with brass wire mesh—the kind of bookcase you might find in a high-toned attorneys' office.

It had originally been purchased by, as it turned out, an attorney for $2,000 and had come into the consignment shop priced at $1,000 but hadn't sold. After a couple of months on the display floor, it was down to $500. We asked the shopkeeper to call the owner and ask if he'd take $400, which he gladly did. We took it on the spot.

About a year later, we'd moved across the country to much smaller digs and didn't have room for the big bookcase, so we put it up for sale and found an immediate potential buyer. We hauled it out of our storage space and stood it up in the
> page 87

If you like the piece, its age doesn't really matter—except for the price. A brand-new reproduction should go for less than a 100-year, old reproduction, which in turn will be far less expensive than a 200-year-old one. But a 50-year-old reproduction—not old enough to really count as an antique—can be less pricey than the brand-new piece. Go figure.

So you need to know what you're looking at. If you're not sure, ask. Most antiques dealers will cheerfully explain the history of the piece to you. If they won't, you might want to take your business elsewhere. How else do you learn? Information on antiques abounds. Take classes at local colleges and adult learning centers or from major antiques houses. Read books and magazines. The Home & Garden channel and PBS carry terrific programs about how to identify and appraise antiques.

Expedition Tip

Although you can find lots of fantastic buys on build-it-yourself furniture at the home improvement or discount store, a vintage piece will hold its value far longer. You can pass it down to your kids and even great-great-grandkids to enjoy, long after that particle-board piece has disintegrated.

Mall mania

Inexperienced bargain hunters tend to get excited when they come across an antiques mall, which features scores of individual dealers all gathered under one roof. All those aisles of goodies! But in our experience, the antiques mall is not always such a hot deal for the bargain-bound.

One reason is that antiques malls provide sales clerks, who aren't necessarily antique-savvy, as part of the lease price for the space. The dealers themselves become absentee shopkeepers. You can't ask questions about an item you want and you can't do any haggling.

The other reason is that dealers who set up displays at these malls tend to be inexperienced part-timers instead of full-time professionals who have their own shops and really know the business. Mall dealers, who often don't have a feel for their wares, look up new acquisitions in a pricing guide and mark their tags accordingly.

This is not a bad tactic (in fact, if you want to learn the antiques trade, it's a good idea to get your hands on a pricing guide yourself), but it doesn't take many of the vagaries into account—the condition of the piece, regional tastes, and what the local market will bear.

How do we know all this? We used to have a space at an antiques mall ourselves. We had a ball. There's nothing quite like having a legitimate reason to go out antiques-hunting. But we quickly discovered that a collectible that would easily fetch $25 in Southern California would gather dust for weeks in Northwest Florida, even if you marked it down to $5. So although we were marking things at a reasonable price for L.A. (that's Los Angeles) and looking them up in the Kovel's Pricing Guide, we couldn't *make* people buy them in L.A. (that's Lower Alabama/Northwest Florida).

Don't take any of this to mean that all antiques dealers at malls are inexperienced and over-priced or that you shouldn't bother shopping the malls. You can have fun and like in any other shopping spot on the planet, if you're a smart bargain seeker you can steal some deals. The best way is to ask the salesclerk to call the dealer and find out if he'll take less. Often the answer will be yes—like the consignor, he's either weary of it sitting on the display floor or he's already left word at the sales desk that he'll take 10 to 20 percent under the marked price.

Expedition Tip

Prices on antiques can vary tremendously in different regions of the country. When you shop an area steeped in tradition and renowned for its history,

B A R G A I N
H U N T E R ' S
J O U R N A L

< page 85

bed of our trusty pickup truck. Just as we were unloading it to show the buyer, it fell off the truck, smashing its *pièce de resistance*, the shell-and-scroll pediment. The buyer decided he didn't want it after all.

So back the bookcase went into storage. When we moved yet again, to Florida, and had enough space, we set it up in the living room. Rob pieced the shell together with wood glue, but the damage was still obvious. So he painted it.

Our Avon lady had a fit when she came in and saw the beginnings—a thick layer of white going over that gorgeous fruitwood. But she didn't stick around for the end result. The interior is still dark-stained wood, but on the outside our bookcase is a lovely glossy white. The shell-and-scroll motif is executed in peach, green, and blue (colors that complement the living room) with gold accents on the shell, base, and doors. Everybody who sees it loves it.

The point here is that you can take damaged goods and with the application of no more than a little glue, a little paint, and a dollop of imagination, turn them into something really special.

such as the fine stores in old Charleston, South Carolina, for instance, you'll find prices that are far higher than just across the bridge in suburban Mt. Pleasant.

Mysteries of the tag codes

Antiques dealers have their own secret codes—right on the price tag—to tell them how they've priced each piece and how long it's been either gracing their showroom or collecting dust. If you can decode these cryptic labels, you'll know just how low the dealer is willing to go.

First you need to know how they do it. A common method is to take two words that equal 10 letters. Each letter stands in for a number from one through 10, such as:

M O N E Y T A L K S
1 2 3 4 5 6 7 8 9 0

This code tells the dealer how much was paid for the piece. For instance, a tag marked MS means that $10 was spent to put that item out on the floor. If you see something marked MSS, you can figure that $100 was paid out.

If the item is priced between $150 and $300 and you see a 3-digit code with two matching end numbers, those two numbers are probably 55 or 00. You'll have to look at a lot of tags to break the code, but it can be done. For instance, if you find a collectible priced at $10 and marked with a Y, you can figure that Y is 5, because dealers often double the price of an object.

All you have to do is come up with two words that total 10 digits (no two letters the same) and you'll have broken the code.

Codes also often contain numbers to remind the dealer of when the piece came into the store. Sometimes it's an obvious date, like 033199 for March 31, 1999, and sometimes it's more cryptic, like the letter code used for the purchase price. You might see something like this: MYY-NNMKK, which would be $155 on 3/31/99.

Once you've broken the code, use your knowledge as a negotiating tool. When you know what the dealer has invested, you can hazard a guess as to how much he can discount and still make a profit. When you know how long it's been on display, you've got a good idea of how anxious the dealer might be to see the last of it.

CHAPTER FIVE Service Providers- The Bargain Hunter's Sidekicks

You can buy more than merchandise by bargaining—everything from plumbing to pest control, airline seats to a seat in the dentist's chair. Sometimes it feels as if you're at the mercy of the insurance company, the auto mechanic, and the plumber, but you're not. Like shopping for products, when you shop for services you're the one in the catbird seat.

Service providers want your business and in most cases, they're ready, willing, and able to work with you in order to get it. So just as you do with retailers, make bargain buddies with these service people and get deals on all sorts of things.

Secrets of the service techs

Need a plumber, gardener, or auto mechanic? You can bargain for their services—or for any other service provider's—just as you can with retailers. Obviously, you're not going to find a marked-down plumber sitting on a shelf, or a damaged auto mechanic, but you can still haggle.

Finding a reliable and competent auto mechanic ranks right up there with one of the most feared tasks in the life of the average American adult. When it's difficult to find a repair shop you can trust, who has the energy to think about bargaining? You need to have it. As a savvy bargain hunter, you can accomplish both with, as the Aussies say, no worries, mate.

Grab that socket wrench and try these tips:

Lean into a learning curve. Vocational and technical schools that train the auto mechanics of tomorrow are delighted to have patients to practice on, for a small fee or free of charge. You get a professional job overseen by a skilled instructor; the students get the experience. Everybody wins! If your job's minor, you might even check it into a high school auto class.

Shop around. For routine tasks such as brake or shock installation, or tire mounting and rotation, you've got to shop around. Some repair centers will provide the installation for free if you buy the parts from them, but others won't. Make your calls first to find out.

Shop even more. If you're taking your car in for major surgery and you don't already have a trusted mechanic, take it to two different shops for two different diagnoses. If they're both the same, go with the better price or better shop. You can also take the lower price to the better shop and ask them to match it. (What if the diagnoses don't match? Call around for more opinions.)

Make pals with the mechanic

Your best bet for good old-fashioned haggling is to make friends with the mechanic. Not the grease monkey who's paid five bucks an hour to crawl under the car and look for oil drips, but the head mechanic. He's the one who knows what he's doing and he's the one you want tinkering under your hood. Talk to him in depth about your car and its problems, just as you'd talk fridges or computers with the department manager down at the retail store.

If you relax and let the mechanic be himself, you should be able to tell if he's honestly interested in your auto or just greasing his palms, what his level of experience is, and what repair route he plans to take.

Now you've found a mechanic you can trust and to whom you can return on a regular basis. Start haggling. Listen to his recommendations, ask what his price will be, then ask if he can do a little better. If the answer is no, press a little harder. Will it be less expensive if you provide the parts? Can he suggest any portion of the program that can be deferred for a short time so the whole expense doesn't come out of your pocket at once? Would it be better if you took your car to a specialist for this particular problem?

The painter in the tuxedo

Along with the auto mechanic, the contractor and his colleagues—the plumber, the electrician, and the painter—are dreaded as people who'll take your money, do a sloppy job, leave with the work half-finished, and with you holding the bag. Not necessarily so.

As partners in a real estate development and property management company, we've seen our fair share of contractor crooks. However, we've seen far more good guys who are out there to make an honest living and help you while they're at it.

The best way to find an ace service tech—from the remodeling contractor right down to the lawn maintenance man—is the same way you find that marvel of a mechanic. Shop around, get a variety of estimates, ask for references (which you need to check—don't be one who doesn't bother), make buddies, and then start negotiating.

Keep these handy tips in mind as you go:

Do a background check. Make sure the contractor has a license in your town or county. Call the building department and get the full skinny on him—have they worked with him on many jobs? What's his reputation? You can also call the Better Business Bureau to see if any complaints have been filed.

Make sure he's covered. Find out if he's got worker's compensation insurance and ask to see proof of the policy.

Give him the once-over. Nobody expects the plumber or painter to appear in a tuxedo, but if he shows up in dirty, torn clothes driving a ratty paint-splattered, rusty, or dirty vehicle, he probably isn't going to take any better care of your job than he does of himself.

Marks the Spot

One of the best places to shop for a variety of services is with the new kid on the block. Find a provider who's new in town or who's just set up shop—they'll be more likely to bargain because they need the business. You get a discount; they get a stellar reference. Another win/win situation! (If they've just come into town, check references from their previous location.)

Expedition Tip

You can often save money on lots of different services if you pitch in. Sometimes it's cheaper if you can provide labor on some types of home repair or landscape jobs. (You know this—you've watched Bob Vila.) You can certainly provide the materials you've bargained for—from kitchen cabinets to ceramic floor tiles—and pay only for labor.

Dr. Bargainstone, I presume

Contrary to popular thought, most doctors are real people. Especially in today's cutthroat world of HMOs and regulations that take funds away from them, most doctors can easily empathize with your desire to keep a few pennies in your pocketbook.

Whether you're a doctor or a patient, health-care costs in this country are all tangled up in the way insurance companies pay for services. Before we go any further, you need to understand how insurance companies pay for health care.

Many insurance plans (Medicare is just one example) set approved rates for various doctor and hospital visits, and procedures. You go to your local doctor's office for an electrocardiogram (EKG). If your doctor *accepts assignment* from your insurance carrier, that means he'll take the amount the insurance plan has decided an EKG and office visit is worth (let's make it $200). That's all he can bill. You probably also have a plan in which the insurance company pays 80 percent, or $160, and you pay the other 20 percent, or $40.

If your doctor doesn't accept assignment, meaning he doesn't want to take the insurance company's approved rate, he doesn't have to. He can charge you 15 percent above that rate if you've got Medicare, and more than that if you don't. Your insurance company, however, will still only pay 80 percent of the approved amount. Now that $200 plus 15 percent is $230, and you're still responsible for 20 percent.

The world of health care is a healthy one in this country. According to the Health Care Financing Administration, Americans spent more than $1,035 billion on health care services in 1996, the most recent year available. That's a lot of aspirin!

What's up, doc?

Okay, enough with the math. The point is that the price of your visit is often dependent on what kind of insurance you have and whether your doctor chooses to agree with the rates. If you don't have health insurance, you can potentially pay even more, not because your doctor is out to cheat you but because he's trying to earn a living for himself.

Look at it this way: If your doctor feels his EKG and office visit are worth $300, but he wants to help out his Medicare or other insurance patients, his hands are tied. He can't take more than $200 or $230. But he can charge his uninsured patients the whole $300.

Here's how *you* bargain these costs, whether you've got insurance or not:

- *I'm pretty healthy. I don't plan on being in here much, so I'm never going to meet my deductible for this year. It would help me out if you let me pay what the insurance company would have paid and call it even.*
- *It looks like I'm going to be in here a lot. And it's going to cost me. It would help me out if you'd take the insurance company's portion as payment in full.*
- *I don't have any insurance. Can I get the starving writer's discount?*

Regarding the last of the above, our dentist's immediate response was "Yes!"

reasure Chest Trivia

According to the U.S. Census Bureau, 85 percent of Americans were covered by some sort of health insurance in 1996, the most recent year available: Group health (61 percent), Medicare (13 percent), and Medicaid (12 percent).

Hold the x-rays

Don't wait until after your doctor has worked his magic to start negotiating payments. Find out at the beginning of a visit or procedure what your costs are likely to be, and then take it from there. As we said, doctors are human. If you're up-front with them, they'll help you out.

BARGAIN HUNTER'S JOURNAL

• Library skills •

Why spend big bucks on the latest spine-tingling suspense novel (or any other new book) when the library can provide it for free?

Our friend, Krista Turner of Normal, Illinois, put her bargain hunting skills to work to procure a copy of a hot new novel. Instead of heading to the bookstore, she took her request to the library. They didn't have the book in inventory. Krista pointed out that it was a good new release and convinced the staff to order it. Then she put her name on the request list. When it arrived at the library, she was the very first to read the brand new copy.

• 2 for the price of 1 •

Jane Hogan of Panama City Beach, Florida, had the misfortune to come down with a bad case of bronchitis while on vacation miles from home. She went to a doctor and at his request had chest x-rays taken, then scheduled another visit so he could review the x-rays and suggest treatment.

When Jane returned home two months later, it was with another bad case of bronchitis. Knowing she'd have to get an x-ray and pay for two doctor visits, she got the x-ray first and brought it with her. One payment instead of two.

Try something like this:

I can't afford full mouth x-rays on top of cleaning and fillings. Do you think we could just x-ray the part that's giving me trouble today and do the rest on my next visit?

You should never ask, or expect, a doctor or dentist to skimp on necessary procedures. Just as you do with the department manager down at the home improvement warehouse or computer emporium, enlist him as an ally.

Expedition Tip

Do your bargaining with the doctor, not the nurse or assistant. The doctor is the one with the authority in the office, as well as the one who's ultimately providing the service.

Save The ER for TV

Some people overspend on health care by paying for more than what they need. Don't let this happen to you. Follow these Handy Health Care Tips to save on doctor bills:

Save the ER for TV. It's amazing how many people go to the emergency room for things like sore throats and stomach flus when they not only wait hours to be seen but then pay through the nose. An ER doctor doing a Level 1 exam, which is a short evaluation, accrues hospital charges on the order of $94. That doesn't include the doctor's bill, which can be another $40 or more, so you pay at least $134. On the other hand, you can go to a walk-in clinic and pay $70 to $80 for a first visit or $55 if you're a repeat patient, or see your own doctor and pay $45. These fees, of course, have wide variations, but this should give you a good cost comparison. Bottom line: Save the emergency room for real emergencies.

Expedition Tip

Just as at the retail store, cash is king. If you can pay your doctor immediately so he doesn't have to wait on the insurance company, then you're doing him a favor.

Call your doctor instead of going in. If you've seen your doctor or dentist several times for a chronic condition or have been in recently, you can often call and ask a question instead of paying a visit. The trick is to call in the morning, if you can, and call again if you haven't heard an answer by noon. Doctors are hard to pin down and their staff can't always grab hold of them long enough to ask your question. If you call again, it lights a fire under the receptionist or nurse and helps get a speedier response.

Ask your pharmacist. Pharmacists are terrific sources for help with over-the-counter remedies for colds, flu, sore throats, rashes, and the like. They'll cheerfully help, either in the store or over the phone, and their advice is far cheaper than going to the doctor.

Let common sense be your guide. All of the above are intended as tips for non-serious situations. You should always let common sense be your guide. If you're dealing with something you're pretty certain is a simple case of sniffles or the 24-hour flu, fine. Don't let saving money stand in the way of seeking the proper medical attention for something that might be serious.

Marks the Spot

Naturally you want your dentist or doc to be an old experienced pro, capable of handling whatever health horrors might arise. But if you're interested in penny-saving and you're talking family practice instead of something like cardiac transplant, check out the new kid on the block. Brand-new practitioners bring with them the latest in training, a fresh, eager attitude, and—most importantly for the bargain hunter—they need patients and are more eager to let you help set their fees.

Apothecary advisors

As long as we're "at" the pharmacy, let's talk medications. Your pharmacist is another major health care ally who often knows more about drug side effects and interactions than a doctor does, so take advantage of his apothecary advice.

When you get a new prescription filled, be sure to ask how you take it—with food, on an empty stomach, frequency, etc. It may seem like simple advice, but many people don't do it, ending up back at the emergency room or doctor's office.

Make sure, too, that you ask your pharmacist to double check that your prescription doesn't interact adversely with something you may already be taking. You might end up paying for a prescription that you later learn you can't use. In many cases, a generic drug is just as potent and just as effective as the name brand. Ask your pharmacist's opinion, and if he says the generic will work, go for it. You'll save a bundle.

Sometimes different strengths of the same drug have far different costs. For instance, a 20 milligram pill can cost less than a 10 milligram one. Ask your pharmacist before he fills your bill if this might apply. If so, he can give you half as many of the larger dosage. Then you buy a nifty little device that cuts pills in half (cost: about $3) and take a half pill instead of a whole one. (Of course, as with all pharmacological tips, get your pharmacist's approval before you do this.)

Expedition Tip

When your doctor writes you a new prescription, ask if he's got free samples he can give you. (He often gets them from pharmaceutical company salesmen.) You can try a week or so of samples and if they work, you fill the prescription. If you experience an allergic or other adverse reaction, you'll find out before having that expensive prescription filled.

Enigmas of the insurance world

Since we've dipped into the intricate world of health insurance, let's expand our coverage a bit and explore the enigmas of the auto insurance world. If you have a car, you know that insurance rates can vary widely, just as in the health care arena. While you can't do much in the way of deep-down haggling, you do hold some bargaining chips, and there are ways to get your rates down to as rock bottom a level as possible.

Find out from your insurance agent what discounts you may be eligible for. Some agents will offer these goodies when they write the policy. With others, you don't know unless you ask:

Not a chimney. If you don't smoke, you can probably light up a tidy discount.

The fleet plan. Many insurers will give you a package deal discount if you have more than one vehicle insured with them.

Bonus for years of service. You can often get a discount for having been a customer with the same company for a number of years.

Stellar student. You may get a price break for being a full-time student.

Safe as houses. Most insurance companies reward you with discounts if your car comes equipped with safety features such as air bags, anti-lock brakes, and anti-theft systems.

Accident-free. You'll also be rewarded for having so many years of accident-free or minimal-damage driving.

On the defense. You may get a break for taking an approved defensive driving course.

More mature. Auto insurers will often reduce your rate once you pass a magic age, like 21 or 25, because they figure you're now more mature and a safer driver.

Just a Sunday driver. If you have a van outfitted as a camper with stove, fridge, and beds, and it's not your only set of wheels, ask your agent to write it up as a motor home. Because insurance companies figure these are driven infrequently, your rate will be lower.

The home office. If you work at home, you can get a discount because you'll drive your vehicle less than someone who has to commute every day.

You don't have to wait until you get a new car or write a new policy to qualify for these discounts. If you or a family member celebrates a birthday, starts off for school, or begins telecommuting, for instance, call your agent and ask him to make a change to your policy.

Expedition Tip

You can often get these same kinds of discounts on your homeowner's insurance. Just ask!

Knock wood

There are other subtle ways in which you can negotiate a rate with your insurance company. If you and your family are safe drivers and you don't—knock wood—anticipate accidents in your future, you may want to raise your deductible.

Why? The higher the deductible, the lower the premium. This could be a good idea if your car is elderly enough that in the event of an accident it wouldn't be worth repairing anyway or if you feel financially secure about footing a bigger deductible if an accident does occur.

Check to see what else you may be paying for with your premium. Some policies automatically provide towing services, but if you belong to an auto club like AAA or Good Sam's, you're double-covered. You can cancel the "free" towing.

E xpedition Tip

One extra you may want to pay for is rental car assistance. For typically less than $20 per year, your insurance company will pay for several weeks of rental car use if your vehicle is not driveable after a wreck.

One instance it really pays to haggle with your insurance company is if you do have that heart-stopping accident, especially if your car is a senior citizen and is totaled or badly damaged. At that point, the insurer may not want to pay you what the car was worth.

However, it is possible for you to get them to cough up what they owe you. Here's what you do:

- Make it clear at the outset that the amount is unacceptable.
- Don't let them send you a check until you've agreed to the amount.
- Look through your local newspaper, shopper, or Auto Trader for cars of the same model and vintage as yours.
- Make copies of the ads and send them to the claims department with a letter explaining that these demonstrate the market value of your car, and the amount you will accept.

This should be all it takes to do the trick. Once they see that you're a savvy negotiator, they should see it your way as well. If not, let them know you'll be taking the matter to your state insurance commissioner.

E xpedition Tip

It pays to bargain, but not to skimp. Make sure you've got the proper coverage for your situation and your family. Enlist your agent as an ally!

Master or mistress of the MasterCard

Just about everybody has credit cards these days, and they're terrific—while you're shopping with them. But when it comes time to pay the bill, you realize that fun little plastic rectangle comes with plenty of strings attached. There's the interest and the finance charges and the annual fees—all sorts of charges tacked onto a bill you thought was only going to show your unfortunate lapse down at the CD & Chocolate Emporium.

As a bargain hunter, however, you can have the last word. You *can* haggle with credit card companies and save money. Follow along as we unlock the mysteries of plastic.

◆ reasure Chest Trivia

Of all of those CD purchases, what's the most popular type of music? According to the Recording Industry Association of America, in 1997 it was rock at 32.5 percent, followed by country at 14.4 percent, and R&B at 11.2 percent.

The huge array

There's a huge array of credit card companies out there vying for your attention and your spending power—about 6,000 by recent count. That's a lot of plastic! This gives you bargaining power so terrific that banks and other credit card merchants will work hard to give you what you want. In many cases, all you have to do is ask.

Let's say you've had a Third Planet BankCard for years. You're pretty happy with it, but here comes your latest bill and as you read over the statement, you see the annual charge of $50 (right after the great bargain you got on CDs and chocolates). Well, you don't mind paying for the cool stuff you bought, but spending another $50 just for the privilege of using the card isn't so wonderful.

How do you get the credit card company to waive the fee? Try something like this:

You: I've had a Third Planet card for years, and I pay my bills on a consistent, timely basis. But I'm not happy with the annual fee you posted on my statement. I'd like you to waive it.

Customer Service Rep: We'd be happy to do that for you. Just deduct the $50 from your statement.

Sometimes, however, you have to apply a tad more pressure:

Customer Service Rep: I'm sorry, but our policy will not allow us to waive the annual fee.

You: Than I'd like to cancel my card. I've got several others I can use that don't charge an annual fee and I'll go with them instead.

Customer Rep: Let me see what I can do. Can you hold for just a moment? (She leaves you listening to the Muzak version of Rolling Stones hits, but comes back a minute or two later.) We'd be happy to waive that fee for this year only. Just go ahead and deduct the $50 from your statement.

By the way, don't worry about the one-time only routine. You can call again next year and do the same thing. And it will work then, too!

Hunting for interest rates

Let's say you've done some A-plus bargain hunting, you've found a cool package deal down at the office supply superstore—computer, printer, copier, and scanner—and you're about to head on over to lay your money on the line. It's a steal of a deal, but it's still a stretch, so you're going to put it on your credit card.

Before you pay with plastic, however, you might want do some further bargain hunting—for the best interest rate. Place a call to your credit card customer service center, and say something like this:

You: I'm planning on making a major purchase with my Third Planet card and I'd like to find out if you can give me a better interest rate than the one I've got now.

Customer Service Rep: We've got you at an 18 percent rate right now. How much were you planning on spending?

You: About $3,000.

Customer Rep: We've got a special program I can let you have that would bring your interest rate down to 12 percent for any purchases made over the next six months.

You: Is that the best you can do?

Customer Rep: I'm afraid it is.

At this point you've got three choices. You can take the not-so-hot 12 percent and say thanks, you can decline and attempt the same thing with another card, or you can try this:

You: I appreciate your help with this, but 12 percent isn't going to work. May I speak to your supervisor?

Supervisor: How can I help you?

You: I'm planning on putting a sizable purchase on my Third Planet card and I was hoping you could give me a better interest rate. The representative I just talked with was helpful, but couldn't do better than 12 percent. I'm sure you can see from my record that I'm a good customer, and I'd rather spend my money with you than put it on my Fourth Galaxy card. Can you help me out?

Supervisor: We could do a 9.9 percent permanent rate.

You: I just got a card offer in the mail promising 4.9 percent. Can you match that?

Supervisor: I can do 4.9 percent for six months, which will then revert back to your current 18 percent, or I can give you 9.9 percent unlimited.

You (thinking 'what's a card holder to do?'): I'd like it better if you could do both.

Supervisor: Okay, we'll do it, but you have to make your purchase within 48 hours.

You: That sounds perfect. Will it be in effect by the time I go to make my purchase this afternoon?

Supervisor: I'll make the change to your account now.

You: Thank you!

Now you've not only gotten a fabulous deal on all that electronic equipment, but you've also negotiated a bargain on those credit card payments.

On the Titanic

What else can you deal on with the credit card people? How about getting them to waive a late charge or a finance charge—or both? You can! The secret again is to just ask. However, you have to be a good customer to begin with. If you're a procrastinator who's always late paying bills, this tactic won't do you any good. Assuming your credit history is good, here's how you handle it:

You: I noticed you posted late charges on my current statement.

Customer Rep: That's because we didn't receive your payment until the 29th and it was due on the 25th.

You: I know. I had to go out of town unexpectedly and I didn't get back in time to put it in the mail. OR I've been working on a killer deadline project and to be honest, I didn't mail it until the 24th. But you can see from my record that I'm a good Third Planet customer and I usually pay right on time. Can you waive the late fee and the finance charge?

Customer Rep: We'd be happy to do that for you. Just deduct those charges from your bill.

You: Thank you!

It's that simple. You don't have to make up a melodramatic story about a death in the family on board the *Titanic*—the truth works fine. The only trick is that you do have to be a good customer.

King Midas drools

You know all those fantastic credit card offers you get in the mail every week? The ones that promise a low, low introductory rate, no annual fee for the first year, and so many freebies that King Midas would drool with envy? Look them over carefully before you decide to run with one.

First, that incredibly low rate only lasts for a few months—which can speed by faster than you'd believe possible—and then you're stuck with a card that has the same rates as the ones you already have.

Second, all those freebies sound spectacular—and they should. Some direct marketing expert toiled for hours to make them appear special. They probably aren't anything different than what your current cards offer. If you're unsure, call the appropriate customer service centers for your cards and ask.

Third, some of those seemingly bargain-basement interest rate cards have a major flaw: They may not give you a *grace period*, which is the amount of time you have (generally 20 to 25 days) to pay your balance without incurring interest. If you don't have a grace period, you'll be charged interest on everything you buy from the minute you sign the charge slip.

Fourth, you can bargain with the cards you already have. Inform you're current card accounts that you've received a wonderful offer you'd like them to match or you may have to cancel your card and switch to a new one.

Too many cards spoil the broth

Having a small selection of credit cards to choose from in your wallet is a good idea. It gives you the bargaining power to cancel one if the company doesn't comply with your requests and still have another one or two on tap. But too many cards—like too many cooks—spoil the broth.

On a personal level, the more cards you have, the more you're likely to spend. Some experts recommend that you stick to one card per person or two per household (one for you and one for your significant other to use.)

If you have a business, you'll want to have a third credit card for business purchases—it's far easier to track expenses when your company has its own card than trying to separate business expenses from pleasure.

On a credit level, mortgage lenders and other picky types who decide if you're worthy enough for that loan look at credit cards not as proof that you're capable of obtaining credit but as a scenario for disaster. In their eyes, each card and its available credit limit is an opportunity for you to go on a spending frenzy.

If you've got 10 cards with available credit of $10,000 each, for instance, the mortgage company sees you suddenly buying $100,000 worth of goodies and running off to Belize, leaving them holding the bag on your house payments. Bottom line: Don't be tempted by every tender offer that arrives in your mailbox.

E xpedition Tip

Just because you've got several cards doesn't mean you should keep them all easily accessible—that's putting temptation in your own path. Choose one and stash the others in your safe or other secret spot. You can pull them out if you need them.

T reasure Chest Trivia

What's the difference between a credit card and a charge card? A *charge card*—like the venerable American Express card—lets you charge purchases but insists that you pay the balance in full when presented with the monthly statement. On the other hand, a *credit card*, lets you charge those purchases and make monthly payments.

Bargain air

Whether you're a footloose and fancy-free type who loves nothing better than to explore new (or old) civilizations or an armchair traveler for whom Sioux Falls is adventure enough, sooner or later you'll want to purchase airline tickets. Talk about strange new worlds! The airline industry is fraught with intricacies, misconceptions, and misleading information designed to thwart the bargain hunter.

Not to worry. There are ways for the traveling woman or man to find terrific airline deals. You just have to know how and where to look.

Airline fares are as changeable as an April breeze and less predictable. Ideally, carriers base their pricing on having every seat of every flight filled, and to that end, they're constantly tinkering with current rates. It's the equivalent of the supermarket bringing the cost of cauliflower up or down several times a week depending on how many heads have been sold in a given time period.

Try these high-flying tips for finding better fares:

Fly during the doldrums. The traditional dead zones for airline travel are mid-week days or the middle of the night. This is because most business travelers—the ones airlines love because they fly on expense accounts—are winging their way out of town on Mondays and returning on Fridays. Saturdays are also doldrum days for airlines, so if you can make your travel week begin on Tuesday, Wednesday, or Saturday and end on a similar day, you can get a better price.

Take Saturday off. Airlines will also give you a better price if you stay over on a Saturday for the same reason. They're banking on the fact that people who spend a Saturday out of town will usually return on a hard-to-book Sunday.

Plan ahead. Airlines will reward you for making your reservation at least three weeks in advance so they're assured that your seat will be filled.

Go for the big bump. If you're not in a hurry and you've brought a good book, get yourself bumped. All you do is show up at the departure gate with your ticket in hand and offer to stay behind in the event of overbooking. Monday mornings are ideal for this ploy, but you can do it any time—the worst that can happen is that you don't get bumped. And the best? By law, you get a refund of up to $200 off your original ticket price if the airline doesn't provide a replacement flight within an hour. Or even better, you get coupons for free flying time to use in the future.

Avoid the hub. You can sometimes negotiate a lower fare by flying into a smaller airport rather than demanding the hub. If you're traveling to Los Angeles, for instance, you can ask about fares into Burbank, Ontario, or John Wayne (Orange County) airports—smaller ports of call that don't get as many seats booked.

Don't think dinky. Conversely, don't insist on a regional airport that's too small to be serviced by more than a couple of airlines. You'll pay extra big bucks for the privilege of landing closer to home. Instead, extend your travel plans and drive the distance to a larger airport.

Keep asking. Don't take the first price the ticket agent quotes you. Ask if they can do better. Give them a hand by being as flexible as possible with departure and destination airports and dates, and keep revising your options until you find one that sounds reasonable.

Marks the Spot

If you don't enjoy the thrill of the chase of airline ticketing (or even if you do), try going through a travel agent. These people can often negotiate better deals than you can—especially for international trips with numerous stops.

Expedition Tip

It's more fun to be mature! Many airlines give seniors age 62 and over discounts of 10 percent or coupon books for discount travel. Call the airline of your choice and ask what programs they have available.

**B A R G A I N
H U N T E R ' S
J O U R N A L**

• Half price happiness •

Because we live in Florida and our families live in Los Angeles, we've found that driving six hours to Atlanta to rendezvous with them during their Georgia business trips is far less costly than driving or flying to L.A. And a heck of a lot of fun! Suburban Atlanta offers addictive, quality antiques shops.

We recently decided it might be fun to stay at a mid-price hotel near the convention center. We called the toll-free reservations number and told the representative we wanted a room. The price: $120 per night. Then we asked if they were running any specials. We were told they happened to have a special discount rate of $63 per night. Wow! Half price, and all for the asking.

Then we called the front desk of a similar lodging in Marietta, a nearby suburb of Atlanta. Their quoted price was $89, but when we reminded them that we'd stayed there two months earlier for only $54, they decided they could give us that rate again. Guess which one we picked?

The bucket shop

Another spiffy way to get cheap tickets is by going through a consolidator. This is a company that arranges to buy a bunch of tickets from an airline at a wholesale price, then turns around and sells those same tickets to you for a marginal mark-up. In Britain, a consolidator is called a bucket shop. (These are the same people who refer to waking you up in the morning as "knocking you up".)

Once upon a time, consolidators were considered to be shady operators because they undercut what used to be federally regulated rates. Now that things have been deregulated, some people remain convinced that consolidators are on the slick side. Actually, most of them run highly reputable companies, although a few—as in any industry—can take your money and run. To maintain your personal security, pay by credit card and check with the airline to make sure your flight's been booked.

Even with the most trustworthy consolidator, there is one way you can run into trouble: If the airline cancels or delays the flight, it won't put you up in style at a hotel or transfer you to another carrier like it would if you'd paid its retail price.

You'll find consolidators on the Internet, in the yellow pages under "Airlines, Wholesale Tickets," or in all those intriguing ads in the Sunday newspaper travel section.

Marks the Spot

Consider an *affinity* card that gives you air miles for you, your business, or both. Many credit card issuers provide cards that give you points for dollars spent. When you reach a certain limit (usually 25,000 points, or $25,000 spent), you get a free airline ticket to anywhere in the 48 contiguous states. Foreign travel requires more points (usually 65,000). You can put just about anything—even groceries—on your card, and as you know, it all adds up fast!

In with the innkeeper

Most people rely on a hotel's toll-free operators to give them the best rates. As a bargain hunter, you should know the top secret of hotel reservation systems—go to the source. It's well worth that long-distance call to talk directly to the hotel's front desk instead of a reservations clerk who's possibly thousands of miles from the scene.

Hotel rates, like airline prices, bounce up and down with the head count. When there's a convention in town and everybody's just about booked solid or when it's tourist season and the hotel's feeling flush, the rates are high. When things get slow, prices become extremely negotiable.

◆ reasure Chest Trivia
The "regular" rate, the one you'll get quoted if you don't ask for a better one, is called by those in the biz *the rack rate.*

An 800-number operator in Omaha, Nebraska, has no idea how many vacant rooms there are in Lake Oswego, Oregon, and probably doesn't care. That's why you need to make that call directly.

Follow these tips for getting a great rate:

Just ask. Often that's all it takes. If you've been to the hotel before and gotten a special rate, let the desk clerk know and ask for the same rate again.

Name drop. Most hotels and motels offer a 10-percent discount or more if you belong to the military, are a senior citizen, or a member of AAA, Sam's Club, or Costco.

Go corporate. You can often get a corporate rate for the asking. Be sure to bring your business card with you in case they ask for it.

Prompt a little. If you'll be arriving off-season, prompt the desk clerk. Remind him that his occupancy rate will be low and you'll be helping him out.

CHAPTER SIX The Cyber Bargain Seeker

U p to this chapter, we've skated past the world of e-commerce because, though we're at the dawn of a new millenium with computers on virtually every desk, not everyone is e-savvy. If you're already an e-shopper, you'll find new tips and bargains in this chapter. If you're an online shopping novice, you're in for a thrill.

Virtual bargain hunting is different than bargain seeking in a "real" store, with its own occasional frustrations, its own eccentricities, and its own very definite charms. It can also be every bit as addictive as bargain hunting in person.

So strap yourself into that cyber-bargain seat (or desk chair) and let's go!

Treasure Chest Trivia

What's with all the "e" stuff? "e" as in *e-commerce* means *electronic,* specifically, online.

Zapped out of cyberspace

Many people don't shop online because they think there isn't anything more available on the World Wide Web than there is on Main Street. These same people don't shop online because they think that purchasing products over the Internet is unsafe—that their credit card information is going to be zapped out of cyberspace by hackers. This is not the case at all.

First, the amount of merchandise available on the Internet is astounding. You can shop at a lot of the same stores and mail order houses that you find in the traditional shopping world—everything from Bloomingdale's to Montgomery Ward to Victoria's Secret—plus thousands of Internet-only retailers.

Expedition Tip

According to the U.S. Department of Commerce, Internet traffic is doubling every 100 days, with Web commerce expected to surpass $300 billion by the year 2002.

Second, shopping on the Internet is every bit as safe—perhaps even more so—than shopping at the traditional store. You need to follow a few simple precautions, but that holds true for traditional purchasing methods, too. You don't give your credit card number over the phone unless you know you're dealing with a reputable merchant or service provider. And you don't slap your credit card down on the checkout counter and walk away. (At least we hope you don't.) The same sorts of precautions hold true for e-shopping.

Expedition Tip

A nice thing about shopping by credit card—online or off—is that you cannot be held responsible for charges of more than $50 made by someone who illegally uses your account. This is not, of course, an excuse to get sloppy with your card. You should also read the fine print that comes with it, such as that you must report fraudulent purchases within 60 days of the charges being made.

The *shop now* key

Let's back up and take things from the top. If you're new to the Net, you're probably wondering how online shopping actually works. We could give you all sorts of technical explanations, but that would be like explaining how TVs work when all you really want to know is how to turn the thing on to catch that old Jimmy Stewart movie on Cinemax. You can find lots of terrific books that do a great job of explaining the technical aspects if you're interested—plus, you can buy them online.

You're ready to *shop now*. However, in place of a wallet with cash, check, or credit card and a set of wheels or shoe leather to take you bargain hunting, you set out on your shopping expedition with:

- Computer with modem.
- An Internet service provider or ISP, which connects you to the Net.
- A Web browser such as Netscape Navigator or Internet Explorer that lets you access the World Wide Web.
- A credit card.
- Your bargain-seeking radar.

None of this stuff is complicated or hard to come by. All recently built computers come equipped with a modem. If they don't, you can easily purchase one to add on. New computers usually come loaded with at least one ISP (such as America Online). If yours doesn't, any one of the many ISPs out there will be delighted to sign you up. Ditto for Web browsers.

E xpedition Tip

With a huge amount of ISPs to choose from, you can get as many as 100 free hours of Net surfing time just by asking. Call any of the 800-numbers touted on TV, in magazines, or in your pile of junk mail and sign up. But be careful. If you exceed your freebie hours, you may get charged for as much as $2.95 per minute (and once you're online and shopping up a storm, an hour can seem like a minute). Still, some enterprising souls—like starving students—get free ISP connections for years by switching from one offer to another and then back again.

Once you're online, head for the "store" you want to explore. For instance, if you want a good book, you can go to the Amazon.com website (at www.amazon.com), which bills itself (and rightly so) as the world's largest bookstore, with 2.5 million titles available.

Shop around. Browse categories from cookbooks and mystery fiction to metaphysics, just as you would at the bookstore in the mall. Type in the subject, title or author of a book you'd like to look at, and Amazon.com takes you to it. You can look at the cover, read a synopsis and review, leaf through readers' comments, or get suggestions for other books by the same author. Furthermore, Amazon.com promises up to 40 percent off, not counting the bargain books section, which is even cheaper.

When you find a book you want, you add it to your virtual shopping cart. Then you shop on, adding as many books as you like.

When you've exhausted either yourself or your virtual pocketbook, you click on "proceed to checkout." Here you review your purchases, change quantities if you like, or change your mind about a book and "put it back on the shelf."

At the checkout "counter," you type in your name and address, your phone number, your e-mail address, your very own secret password, and your credit card number. You can also choose gift wrap and the type of shipping you want to use: overnight, 2nd day air, or ground transport.

The checkout "person" totals your charges, adds tax and shipping, and shows you the bill. If you're happy with what you see, you hit the *send* button and you're done. A short time later, you get an e-mail confirming your order and displaying the requisite information you selected.

A day or more later (depending on availability and your shipping choice), you get another e-mail indicating your order's been shipped.

Then, your doorbell rings. It's UPS or FedEx with your books! (and Amazon.com usually sends a free bookmark or post-it notepad, too.)

Expedition Tip

Another great thing about shopping online is that once you've given the Web site your personal info like credit card and shipping address, you never have to do it again unless you change the card you want to use or you move. So every future purchase is quick and easy. (Of course, spending money usually is.)

E-shopping 101

Cyberstores, like "real world" stores, don't all operate alike. You may find departments to browse in are not set up in exactly the same way in other online bookstores, lingerie stores, grocery, or computer stores. Cybershops don't all offer the same amenities in the way of product reviews or descriptions. But like "real world" shopping, the surprises are at least half the fun.

On to e-shopping 101. You can see (we hope) why Internet bargain hunting is so much fun. Let's explain why it's safe. When you send your credit card information through the Web, it's sent through a *secure server,* which *encrypts* it, turning it into long strings of coded numbers, letters, and symbols (like in a Ken Follett spy novel). If the Hacker from Hades somehow tore himself away from trying to disrupt national security and concentrated instead on intercepting your Third Planet card—cracking into the secure server—all he'd get is a jumble of digits, letters, and symbols.

Take this simple quiz. Which do you think is safer:

- Sending your card information over a secure server to an Internet store?
- Giving your card information by phone to a customer service rep at a mail order house?
- Giving your actual card to the guy in the little window at the gas station, who has you sign the charge slip and then watches you drive away while he still has your card number and your signature in his hand?

The major caveat here is that it's your responsibility to make sure the site you're shopping on has a secure server. If it doesn't, *don't give out your card number or any other personal information.* How do you know if it's a secure site? It tells you so in a message window or with an icon (a locked padlock), or both.

Somewhere out there

What can you expect to buy online? Let's revise that question. What *can't* you expect to buy? Here's a small sampling of what you can find: airline tickets, baby food, computer stuff galore (this is, after all, computer shopping), hotel reservations, food, and clothing. Antiques, collectibles, cars, trucks, and Hummers. Boats, bread, gift baskets, fragrances, furniture, and fine art. You can order a Maine potato sampler, hire a private investigator, clip coupons, and bid at auctions. If you can imagine it—and in many cases, even if you can't—it's somewhere out there.

⬥reasure Chest Trivia

By 2003, more than 40 million American households will shop online to the tune of $108 billion in revenues, says Forrester Research's *Retail's Growth Spiral* report.

Bargains ho!

Shop the Web the same way you shop the swap meet or the retail store. Unless you know it's a steal that's going to be snapped up in a flash, you don't grab the first teddy bear you see in the first aisle. You hunt around, poking your nose into every nook, cranny, and cardboard box. You ask questions, get to know the layout of the store or flea market, and make buddies with the salespeople or dealers. Virtual bargain seeking works the same way. You'll find some sites you'll fall in love with and others that will leave you cold, some that offer incredible deals, and others where the pickings are slim.

Okay, we hear you asking, how do you make buddies and haggle when there's nobody to actually talk to? Isn't bargaining a two-way street?

One solution is to combine cybershopping with calling live human beings. We found, for instance, a software sale on the Parsons Technology Web site at www.parsonstech.com and picked out a title we liked. Then we called them at their toll-free number and told the customer service rep which program we wanted to order.

Then came the good part. We'd been coveting a particular clip art program for months, but the price never seemed to budge. So when the customer rep asked if we'd like to order another title from their sale list, we asked if she could give us a better price on the clip art, even though it wasn't on sale. She gave us a 20 percent discount and sent it to us along with the one we'd found online.

Expedition Tip

Before you actually plunk down your virtual money in a Web shopping spree, make sure the site gives a phone number to call in case you've got problems or questions—and of course, for further bargaining.

The virtual shopping bag

This brings us to another point about Web bargain hunting. Because you can't have that virtual sales clerk pop your purchase into a shopping bag, you have to arrange for shipping—and those charges can add up quickly.

Most e-shops give you a choice of shipping methods. Of course, the sooner you want it, the more you're going to pay. If you purchase several products at once (yes, you can bulk buy or make package deals), you save by paying one shipping charge instead of multiple ones. Some Web merchants will give you options. If, for instance, you've ordered one item that's available immediately and another that has to be back-ordered, you can choose to wait for the back-ordered one and have them both shipped at the same time. You can also have one delivered right away and then pay a separate charge for the other one later.

reasure Chest Trivia

Back in 1961, Bloomingdale's, according to the store's Web site, was the first to tout designer shopping bags to tote and collect. The clothes emporium got its start in the 18th century as a purveyor of hoop skirts.

Software: the next generation

But Web shopping gets even better. There *are* some things you can buy and have immediately—without waiting for shipping. It doesn't work with purchasing pizza or perfume, but if you want software and you need it *now*, you can have it. Go for the downloads, which are offered by lots of software e-shops. All you do is pick out the title you want, pay for it, click a few keys, and the program appears on your computer, ready to use.

Even better for the bargain seeker, you can find free software to download. Of course, it's not all going to be the latest version of a super-popular title like RoboKiller Goes to Washington, but you can have your pick of some prime stuff:

Freeware is just what it says, no-cost software that the developer makes available in the hope that he'll catch the eye of a high-paying software publisher.

Shareware is freeware, the next generation. You get to download the program for nothing, but after you've used it for a specified period of time, you're expected to cough up the payment. If you're not nuts about it, you stop using it. Otherwise, every time you get into it, a screen pops up that not-so-subtly reminds you of your obligation. When you pay, the developer gives you a secret software key that disables the *pay me* screen.

Demoware is another version of freebie software. Commercial developers (instead of lone rangers working in basement laboratories) let you download programs to try out. The big difference between demoware and its siblings, free and shareware, is that demoware is basically a teaser. You can access the program, but there is a catch, which is usually one of the following:

- You get all the features you'd find if you paid full price, but you only get to use them for a period of time (typically 30 days) before the program disables itself.
- You can start and run the program a specified number of times (usually 30 to 50) before it self-crashes. If this is the option you get, make sure you only access the program when you're fairly certain you'll have plenty of time to play with it.
- You get frustrated by limitations on what you can do. This version of the demo is called *crippleware* because it cripples an important function like printing or saving, forcing you to abandon the program or buy the full-access version.

Expedition Tip

Whether you choose freeware, shareware, or demoware, be *extremely* careful of what you're downloading and from whom. If you're indiscriminate, you could download nasty computer viruses along with the program, which can effectively crash your system and kill your hard drive. If you're not certain you're downloading from a secure source, don't do it. A freebie isn't worth blowing your system.

Read about it online

It's not just software you find free on the Internet. You'll find online editions of numerous magazines and newspapers. Read your favorite rag without the subscription fee!

Of course, some are abbreviated editions, offering various articles, editorials, and columns, but not everything you'd find in the paper version. (For instance, you don't get those perfume ads with the scented strips you can rub across your wrist.) Others carry a great deal of content. Most come complete with archives so you can root around in the back files without getting pesky newsprint on your fingers.

When you read online versions, you can't clip articles or tear out recipes, but you can easily print them. Plus, you can access goodies you won't find in the paper versions, such as virtual tours of homes in decorating magazines, chat rooms where you talk online to editors or guests, and the ability to send e-mail questions to experts.

Dusty corners of cyberspace

Cybershopping is not just for new and reconditioned merchandise. You can find plenty of pre-loved items online. Like bargain seeking at your neighborhood garage sale or thrift shop, you can poke around in the dusty corners of cyberspace and come up with great stuff. You'll find pre-owned goods in two main places on the Web: the classifieds (just like in your hometown paper) and the auction.

Classified information

Bargain hunting the online classifieds is just like sitting at your kitchen table with your morning java and the daily paper—with a twist. For starters, you'll find ads from all over the country (or even further afield), so you're not restricted to goodies from your relatively immediate neighbors. Of course, if you find something you like, you can't hop in the car and go take a gander, either, but there are ways around that little obstacle.

However, online classifieds often include a handy notification system that lets you know when the object of your affections comes up for sale. For instance, if you just have to have a 1963 G.I. Joe in full Marine battle dress, you tell the system what you want. Then, when an appropriate Joe makes the classifieds, you receive an e-mail alerting you to its availability so you can buy him before somebody else does.

B A R G A I N H U N T E R ' S J O U R N A L

• **Digital exposures** •

While doing realworld shopping at our local office supply superstore, we found a terrific deal on a Kodak digital camera. (We knew it was a steal because we'd adhered to Bargain Seeker's Secret No. 5 and shopped around a lot.) The camera was a demo. We haggled with the store manager and got it down to $350 from the original price of $700.

A week later, while Web surfing, we happened onto the Kodak site and discovered that the legendary camera maker sells reconditioned units at bargain basement prices—the unit we'd bought was only $299 online.

So we called our friendly store manager, told him that we'd found a better price at Kodak, and asked if he would match it. His store policy dictates that customers can return any product within 30 days for a full refund and that the store will price-match. Even though the demo we had in hand was basically brand-new and was being compared to a reconditioned unit, he agreed.

By combining e-shopping with traditional shopping, we got a cool digital camera for less than half price.

Then, what about the fact that you might be in Lake Forest, California, while Joe and his current owner are in Lake City, Florida? Communicate (with the owner, not with G.I. Joe) either by phone or e-mail or both, have the owner give you a description of the toy's condition, or send you photos. Armed with your finely tuned bargain hunter's antennae, you can then decide whether or not you want to give Joe a new home.

If you're worried about sending money to someone you've never seen, you can have them send their picture along with the toy's. But a better way to handle the matter is to have them send your purchase COD. You don't pay until that action figure is in your hands, and the former owner rests assured he'll get his money via the delivery service. You can negotiate over who pays the COD charge and, of course, haggle over the price of the merchandise.

Another route to take is to engage an escrow or transaction service to hang on to your money until you get delivery of the goods. Once you and the seller agree to this step, you send payment to the service, which notifies the seller that you've forked over the dough. The seller then sends G.I. Joe to you, and you get to examine him. When you give your approval, the service sends your payment on to the seller. Escrow services usually charge 5 percent of the purchase price, depending on the cost of the item, or a $5 minimum.

Marks the Spot

As an online ads sampler, circle these spots: Classifieds2000 at www.classifieds2000.com and FreeClassifiedAds.com at www.freeclassifiedads.com.

Auctions away!

For the most part, online auctions work pretty much like those that are up close and personal. However, instead of walking into the barn or backyard, you wend your way inside with your trusty keyboard and mouse, nosing around, seeing what's up for bid, just as you do at live auctions. Of course, rather than items being arranged on tables or under trees, they're set up by categories—antiques, books, collectibles, computers, jewelry, housewares, toys—and you click onto whatever catches your fancy.

For instance, you might be looking for dolls, so you click on Barbie for information such as the starting bid price, the number of bids already made, and the closing date for that particular auction. (At the online auction house, each item or set of items is considered a separate auction with its own opening and closing dates and times. What do we mean by set of items? Multiples of the same thing. For instance, a seller might have a dozen groovy lava lamps he's offering as one auction.)

When you find an item you think sounds intriguing, you click on it and are rewarded with a page devised by the seller, which includes a description of the product and sometimes a photograph. On eBay at www.ebay.com, you also get to read a mini-bio of the seller and view his photo (although not all sellers submit this info), and you get to read comments from people who've bought something from him in the past.

Suddenly you're hooked and ready to bid. (Although now you've switched from the dolls category to collectibles and fallen in retro-love with lava lamps.) First you have to register, which means filling in all the required fields with your name, e-mail address, etc., just like you do when you buy anything else online for the first time.

At some auction sites, you'll enter your credit card information. This is because at some online auctions the site itself owns the merchandise, so you pay them directly. For us, the really enjoyable sites are the ones where the site functions as the auctioneer, but you deal directly with the seller—just as you do when buying from any form of Internet classified ad.

The bid babysitter

So how exactly do you place your bid? Pretty much the way you do at a live auction, but again with a twist. You take a look at the minimum bid price (let's say it's $20 for a lava lamp-print t-shirt), at the bid increments (we'll make it $1), and at the current high bid. Just as at the barn auction, if the current top bidder has upped the price to $30 and you don't think any T-shirt is worth that, you don't bid.

But you're a serious lava lamp aficionado (or about to become one), so you decide to bid. You enter yours, the next person enters theirs, and the race is on. That's sort of all there is to it, because at many auction sites, instead of bidding on a blow-by-blow basis, you enter your maximum bid. If you've decided that you're willing to cough up $45 for an item, that's the number you enter.

Here's the cool part: Once you've set your bid ceiling, you can toddle off and bid on other auctions, shop for a gift for your mom on a different Web site, or go outside and mow the lawn. The auction site takes over for you as a virtual bid babysitter.

If somebody else who's seriously into lava lamps comes along and bids $31, the site will automatically bid $32 on your behalf. If your rival ups the ante to $33, the site bids $34 for you and so on, until it reaches your top limit of $45. If at that point no one bids above you, you win the T-shirt. The site notifies you by e-mail.

But it gets even cooler: If nobody bids above the $34 you offered by the time the auction ends, you get the t-shirt for $34—even though you said you were willing to pay as much as $45. How's that for bargain power?

Going dutch

Another offbeat aspect of Internet auctioning is the Dutch auction. This is put into play when a seller offers multiples of the same item, such as lava lamps. For example: The lamps are offered with a minimum bid of $40 each. You bid $50 for one, another bidder offers $45 for another, and a third offers $42 for 10 lamps. (What's he going to do with them all? Who knows?) You get your lamp for $42 even though you bid $50, because the lowest high bid was $42. And the other bidders—even the guy who wants all 10—get them for $42 each, too.

E xpedition Tip

Just like a "real" auction, if you're the winning bidder at a virtual auction, you're obligated to pay for the merchandise. Make sure the price you bid is one you and your wallet can live with.

E xpedition Tip

Follow the same precautions for purchasing products at auction as you do when shopping the Internet classifieds. Never send cash. Use a cashier's check or money order that can be traced if the seller claims he never received it.

CyberSkies

If you're contemplating a flight through those friendly skies, the Internet is the place to start. You'll find travel bargains galore, plus lots of sites that function as freewheeling journals from explorers all over the globe. Even if you end up going no further than your desk to your favorite armchair (with laptop at hand), you can experience some entertaining, informative, and even bizarre travel adventures.

Marks the Spot

For travel reading that will whet your appetite for cool adventuring and exploring, start with Lonely Planet Online at www.lonelyplanet.com. To get your feet wet without the gonzo stuff, try the more traditional Fodor's Travel Service at www.fodors.com. (If you've noticed that these titles are remarkably similar to those guide books in the travel section of your local bookstore, they are. And you can read them for free.)

Sense and sensibilities

After you've read up on all those fab foreign climes (or maybe just New Jersey) and you want to hop aboard the next jet, you'll want to cybershop air fares. This is where you get to put yourself in the virtual travel agent's seat. Ready?

Click onto a travel booking site such as:

- *Expedia* (expedia.msn.com)

- *TravelWeb* at (travelweb.com)

BARGAIN HUNTER'S JOURNAL

• When you've got to go •

We had to go to Los Angeles and get there in four days, and we'd already flown our frequent flyer miles. But a dear and close family member had passed away and we wanted to be at the funeral, so we put our bargain hunting skills to work.

First we called the airlines and explained our situation. Airlines will give you a special bereavement rate or provide a discount for a family emergency. However, in our case the "special fare" of $1,680 per person from our airport in northwest Florida seemed more astronomical than compassionate.

On to bargain travel tactic number two, the nearest big city or hub, which in our case is Atlanta. This time the fare was $777 per person—a lucky number in Las Vegas but not a bargain. On to travel tactic number three: the Net. First we got onto Travelocity, touted as a supersaver site, and found fares from $1,038 and up. But hopping on over to Cheap Tickets.com, we found round trip fares to L.A. from Atlanta for only $238 each. We had to drive to Atlanta and back, but we used the drive to remember Tim, a wonderful brother-in-law and bargain hunter, too. We think he would have been pleased.

Some sites want you to sign up before they'll let you fare-surf, but that's okay. You won't have bought anything you couldn't return.

Check fares. All air fare sites work in basically the same way. You choose your departure and return destinations, the date you want to travel, airline preference (if any), and whether you want to wing it in coach or snooze above the clouds in luxurious first-class. Then, through the magic of cyberspace, you're presented with several suggested flights and fares.

If you don't find one that's suitable, you can stay on the same site and keep revising your options until you hit the jackpot with a price that fits your pocketbook and your sensibilities.

Keep in mind that you may not find a fare you like on any one Web site. Not to worry. Try another site. In the airline fare world, rates change at Concorde speed and can vary from site to site and day to day, or even hour to hour. When you find one you like, you buy it in the same way you make any other online purchase.Print out your itinerary so you don't forget where you thought you were going and when. A few days later the tickets are delivered to your door or mailbox and you're off!

E xpedition Tip

If you're in a hurry and don't want to wait for delivery, you can sometimes arrange to pick up the tickets at the airport counter or from a local travel agent. You can also go for the *e-ticket*, which is where you get e-mailed a confirmation number instead of a ticket, take it down to the airline boarding gate and check in.

X Marks the Spot

You can shop for hotel rate bargains the same way you shop for air fares, and on the same Web sites. Check into Hotel Discounts at www.hoteldiscounts.com, which promises rates up to 65 percent off and even bookings for sold-out dates.

Fly you to the moon

Yet another method for flying on the cheap is to go the ticket auction route. Besides providing you with rock-bottom fares, this shopping method is a hoot because it makes the airlines and travel agents match your price instead of the other way around.

On the PriceLine site at www.priceline.com, you pre-shop for the best ticket price and choose the lowest one you can find. Then you post your own price and the bidding begins for any airline willing to match the rate you've set. The one that comes closest wins you as a passenger. The whole process takes about an hour.

Don't imagine that you can fly to the moon (or even Half Moon Bay) for $5. The airline people aren't that desperate. You have to be reasonable—the PriceLine folks suggest you set a price that's an established low fare. But as a bargain seeker, you owe it to yourself to fly at as low a rate as you can. Don't err on the over-reasonable side, either.

On the TravelBids site at www.travelbids.com, they run things a little differently. The gimmick here is that you shop around, choose a flight and make your reservation. But don't pay for it! Then you post your choice on the site and wait while travel agents bid on how much of a discount to give you. The winning bid wins you, takes your credit card information, and books the flight, just as if he'd handled the transaction from the beginning. Of course, you get the discount.

Be aware that for most of these sites, you have to pay a $5 registration fee and the winning discounts aren't huge—most are in the 6 to 8 percent range—but a bargain's a bargain. Because the site handles cruises and destination vacations like ClubMed as well—which are more expensive than airline tickets—you can appropriate some solid discounts, especially when they come on top of bargain fares you've already scouted out.

Marks the Spot

Since the airlines live in mortal fear that they'll be caught with unfilled seats, you get the absolute best bargains by traveling at the drop of a ticket. If your schedule is flexible (or if you can twist it until it is), you can grab some great deals. Check out WebFlyer at www.webflyer.com and 1travel.com at www.1travel.com.

CHAPTER SEVEN The Jewel in the Driveway

reasure trove isn't always found on store shelves or in card board boxes at the back of the thrift shop. Sometimes it's out in the parking lot or the driveway. It can be a car, a van, a pickup truck, a sport-utility vehicle, or even a motor home. But whatever name it goes by and however many doors it has, it can be a honey or headache, a lemon or a luscious deal.

Most people—even those who are ace bargain hunters at the flea market—view car buying with the same enthusiasm they reserve for the dentist or the IRS auditor. Car dealers have a well-deserved reputation for being manipulative, underhanded, sneaky, sleazy. Let's be polite and just say they often don't operate with your best interests at heart.

Purchasing a used vehicle from a private party is a car of another color—and another buying situation that makes most people blanche. How do you know you're getting a reliable vehicle and not a rust bucket primed to fall apart as soon as it hits your driveway? How do you know what's a steal and what's not?

Not to worry. The savvy bargain shopper sees an auto purchase as just another adventure. In this chapter, we'll show you how to fine-tune your expertise in the car buying arena, starting with that old arch-nemesis, the new car salesman.

The new car nemesis

Your best tools for dealing with the dealer are the 12 Secrets of the Bargain Seeker, the same ones we've employed throughout this book. You mix in the car dealer's secrets, which we're about to divulge, and you're in the driver's seat.

Dealing with the new car dealer is a bargain seeker's equivalent of hunting dangerous big game. In most of the retail world, sellers are genuinely nice people who want to help you get a good deal—as long as they make a buck, too, they're happy to work *with* you.

But car salesmen are trained to work against you. These fellows are pros armed with every trick in the book to get you to buy at their price.

Pull out Bargain Seeker's Secret No. 1 and don't be shy or intimidated. The bottom line of bargaining holds true on the car lot just as it does at the home improvement store or the flea market.The dealer needs you just as much—or more—than you need him. When you go car shopping, you're giving that dealer an opportunity to move his merchandise—those shiny vehicles are costing him money every day they sit on the lot. You wield a tremendous amount of power merely by walking into the showroom.

◆ reasure Chest Trivia

According to the U.S. Bureau of Economic Analysis, retail sales of new motor vehicles totaled more than 15 million in 1997.

Driving diva

Buying a car is a major investment. Next to real estate, it's probably the second largest purchase you'll make, so this is not the time to be an impulse shopper. Apply Bargain Seeker's Secret No. 5 and shop around.

Just like buying a TV or a refrigerator, you need to look at many different makes and models, and decide what you want. Besides the all-important question of price, think about features: the color for instance, or whether you want a two or four-door, convertible, sunroof or hardtop, automatic transmission or standard, four-cylinder or V6 engine. Are you a driving diva who'll be miserable unless you've got a stereo/CD player package with all the bells and whistles, or would you be happy with a radio and a tape deck? Narrow down your choices as much as possible until you arrive at the ones you feel best about.

Window shop dealerships in your area. Take your time and snoop. Climb behind the wheel. Sniff the leather. Get acquainted with the makes and models on offer.

Expedition Tip

Don't forget Bargain Seeker's Secret No. 4: Make buddies. It's hard to cozy up to a car dealer, but if you act cool, you can pique his attention and have him anxious for your return. Be careful, though! Make it clear you're just looking. Don't get roped into any discussions about pricing, trade-ins, or other monetary matters until the day you come back to buy.

Read all about it. Go to the bookstore, newsstand, or library, and check out magazines like *Car and Driver, Consumer Reports,* and *Road & Track,* which offer reviews of new vehicles, and get the latest stats, facts, and figures on the models that interest you.

Armed and dangerous

When you've decided which vehicle is your dream creampuff, do the last all-important piece of research and find out what the dealer's cost really is. Common knowledge has it that this information is so top secret, not even the CIA has access to it. Not true.

When you know where to look, it's easily available. If you have a computer, get online and go to Edmund's at www.edmunds.com. Now look up the following for the vehicle you've chosen:

- Manufacturer's Suggested Retail Price (MSRP).
- Dealer invoice.
- Dealer holdback.
- Current incentives and rebates.
- MSRP of any options you'd like.
- Dealer invoice on those same options.

If you're planning on trading in your present car, you'll need to look up its trade-in value. If your vehicle is 10 years old or younger, you can find this information on the Edmund's Web site or on the Kelley Blue Book site at www.kbb.com.

Go to the library and look up the new vehicle information in *Edmund's New Car Prices and Reviews, Edmund's New Truck Prices and Reviews,* or *The Consumer's Guide.* Check out your trade-in stats in the Kelley Blue Book or the N.A.D.A. (for National Automobile Dealers Association) Official Used Car Guide. (You can also call your local bank's loan officer, who'll look up the wholesale, or trade-in, price of your car in one of these publications, but bankers generally have copies that only go back seven years.)

Now you're armed and dangerous (at least to the dealer) because you know his secrets. You know how much that beauty sitting on his lot actually cost him and how much bargaining he can afford to do. Let's take a look at the information you've obtained and see what it means:

Manufacturer's Suggested Retail Price, otherwise known as the *MSRP* or *sticker price*. This is just what it says it is—the amount Ford or Chevy or Honda says is a "suggested" price—not a real price. All it really represents is a way for you to figure out the dealer's price.

MSRP on options. Again, this is only a "suggested" price.

Dealer's invoice with options (if you've chosen any). Now we're getting closer to what the dealer paid, but this isn't it, either. Watch: other items get factored in.

Dealer holdback. This is basically a refund from the manufacturer to the dealer. The dealer has to pay the manufacturer up front for any car he puts on his lot, but he gets a percentage of his money back when he sells the car. That amount could be anywhere from 2 to 3.5 percent of the MSRP, although a few dealers, such as Volvo, pay a flat fee, and some others, like Audi and Daewoo, don't give holdbacks at all.

If, for instance, the MSRP with your option package is $20,000, the dealer invoice with his version of the option package is $18,000, and the holdback is 3 percent, you know that the dealer gets $600 when he sells you the car (3 percent of $20,000). Now you take that $600 off of the $18,000 invoice price, and the car is actually only costing the dealer $17,400. Pretty nifty, huh?

The holdback is a vital dealer secret, one that is often not even divulged to the salesmen. Why? Because if the salesman doesn't know, the dealer doesn't have to share it as part of the commission.

But now *you* know, and the mystery of how car dealers can advertise big "blow-out" sales where they sell cars at factory invoice and still make a living is solved. Even if they do sell at invoice, they're earning hundreds of dollars per vehicle.

Current incentives and rebates. These are handed out by the manufacturer to encourage sales on less-popular models. They come in two flavors: customer and dealer. Customer rebates are about the same as the ones you get when you buy anything from software to brandy—you buy the product and the manufacturer gives you back a chunk of change. But in the vehicle arena, you can sometimes choose between a cash rebate and a lower finance rate. Rebates can typically range from $500 to $2,000.

With dealer incentives, there's also a choice involved: whether the dealer wants to give that cash rebate he gets for selling the car to you or hang on to it himself. If he doesn't have a lot of excess inventory to move—which may prompt him to advertise the incentive in another "blow-out" sale and pass the dough along to you—he can keep mum and retain the cash. This is another deep, dark dealer secret that the salesman may not be privy to either, and with good reason—those incentives can range from $500 to $5,500.

But *you* know, so you can subtract this from the dealer's invoice, too. Let's go back to that car with the MSRP of $20,000. We've already knocked the price down to $17,400. Now let's take off another $2,000 for incentive, and we're close to the dealer's real, true cost of $15,400.

Why do we say "close?" Because dealers often get other perks in the form of additional incentives for moving certain models during particular periods, such as when the next year's versions come out.

The eleventh hour

You feel better about car buying already, don't you? Let's check the clock, the calendar, and the Weather Channel for the prime car shopping periods:

End of the day. The best time to hit the dealer is no more than an hour or two before the place closes for the evening. Everybody from the sales manager and the floor salesman to the finance/insurance person is exhausted and ready to call it a night. And a car purchase is not a quick operation. Maneuvering the customer from their initial interest to that signature on the dotted line can take hours. Car salespeople usually use this time to wear down the would-be buyer. But if you show up late, you turn the tables. The longer the whole thing takes, the more concessions they'll be willing to make just to get you out the door so they can go home.

End of the month. Both salesmen and dealers often have quotas to fill that come due at the end of the month. If they sell enough vehicles they get a tidy bonus, so if you arrive at the eleventh hour on the 26th day or later, they may be more inclined to give you a bargain so they can add another notch to their belts and claim that bonus.

Stormy weather. Bad weather doesn't bring in many shoppers, so salesmen are more willing to bargain with you—you're a warm body and if they can't make a fortune off you, they can at least get points toward their quotas.

E xpedition Tip

The worst time of the year for car dealers is the period just before and after Christmas. Shoppers are more interested in gifts they can fit under the tree than one that sits out in the driveway, and desperate dealers are anxious to make a deal.

Talking trade-in

We've time our mission perfectly. It's nine p.m. on a cold, rainy night during the last week in December, or a hot, muggy, drizzly night at the end of July. Now, we still haven't done anything with that trade-in price you researched, but not to worry.

At the showroom, the salesman will want to talk trade-in. This is because car dealers believe that customers are fixed on either a good trade-in price for their old vehicle, or a good deal on a new car. Once they've correctly identified you as an "a" or a "b," the rest is simple. They concede on the trade-in and nail you on the new price, or they offer you zip for your old car and give in a bit on the new one.

As a savvy bargain hunter, of course, you've done your homework. You know your car's trade-in price. They might try to tell you your mileage is too high or the equipment package doesn't qualify for a good trade-in price, or some other tale. But since you've already factored in these variables, you don't need to budge.

T reasure Chest Trivia

Just how popular are those minivans? According to the American Automobile Manufacturers Association, 64,000 cargo minivans and nearly 11 million "mini-passenger carriers" were sold in 1996.

Cherry condition

Why is the dealer so anxious to give you a rock-bottom trade-in price? Because he's planning on making a profit on your car. He'll sell it at a dealers-only auction, sell it directly to another dealer, or sell it on his lot. If he's planning on either of the first two options, he needs to buy it below wholesale in order to sell it at a wholesale price.

If he sells it on his lot to a consumer, he will, of course, get the retail price, which is far higher than the wholesale one. However, it'll cost him more because he has to detail it inside and out, repair any mechanical glitches, get his body shop to bang out any dings, advertise it, pay commissions to the salesman who sells it, and arrange financing and insurance.

So if you can get the Kelley Blue Book trade-in or wholesale value for your wheels, you've accomplished something. The best way to do this is to leave as little as possible for the dealer to do. Bring it to the showroom in cherry condition. Clean all those fast-food wrappers out from under the seats, shampoo the upholstery and carpets, spritz it with car perfume. Wash and wax the exterior and buff up the tires with Armor All.

When the salesman says, "I'm afraid we can't give you full price for your car because we'll have to do a lot of work to it," you bounce right back with "Did you look at the car?" with a full explanation of its great condition.

E xpedition Tip

Look like a player when you go into the showroom. It's not necessary to dress as if you're having tea with the Queen, but your appearance should show that you can comfortably afford the car. Masquerading as a bag lady won't get you a better deal. All that will happen is that the salesman will dismiss you as not worth his time.

The dealer's arsenal

Car dealers are champs at getting you to pay more for that shiny new model than what you thought it cost when you started negotiating. So your job is not only to bargain down from the sticker price (the MSRP), but to avoid being sucked into paying up. You can avoid these pitfalls by keeping in mind Bargain Seeker's Secret No. 7: Be willing to walk away. This works better than just about anything at winning the new car game.

Watch for these tactics in the dealer's arsenal:

Tactic #1: The Go-between. Whenever you and the salesman negotiate a term in the deal, he has to go get the sales manager's approval, and the sales manager always says no, forcing you to concede some point. You think your friendly salesman has left you alone in that tiny cubicle because he's arguing on your behalf with the manager when he's really drinking coffee or filing his nails in the break room. This is just a ruse to wear you down and make you think that in the end—when they've finally gotten you to agree to their terms—you've won when you haven't.

Your solution: Don't fall for it. Use all your bargaining skills and wear them down instead. One of the best tactics we've ever heard came from a listener who called in to the absolutely fabulous National Public Radio show *Car Talk.* This brilliant bargainer reported that each time the sales staff presented her with a price, she said, "Gee, I don't know. I'll have to ask my husband." She'd use their phone to call Hubby at home, who would say into her ear, "That's a great price. Take it!" The bargainer would hang up and tell the car salesmen, "He says it's too much money." So they'd lower the price. She worked this scenario four times until she got them down $2,000 from the original price of the car. Sheer genius!

Tactic #2: The old bait and switch. In this classic ploy, you walk into the dealership expecting to buy a car that was advertised on sale. However, when you approach the salesman, you discover that somebody just bought the last one. Then you're steered into buying a more expensive model.

Your solution: Leave. Not only are there other fish in the sea, there are other dealers in town.

Tactic #3: We lost it. Car salesmen figure the longer they've got you in their clutches, the more opportunity they have to wear you down until eventually you'll agree to any price just to break free. So they frequently "lose" things. They may borrow your keys so they can check out your trade-in and then "misplace" them so you can't leave. Or they might ask for a deposit and then "lose" it so you can't get up in a huff and leave.

Your solution: Don't give them anything to lose. If they want to appraise your car, go out to the parking lot with them. If they want a deposit, refuse to give them money until everything's been agreed upon by all parties and you're ready to sign on the dotted line.

Tactic #4: The Lowball. This works pretty much like the bait and switch, except that the salesman quotes you a wonderfully lowball offer on your dream car and then, once he's got you twitching to get behind the wheel, says you don't qualify because of your credit rating. Then you're pressured into buying something more expensive.

Your solution: Walk. Again, there are many dealers and many cars out there. You're not under obligation to anyone.

Car salesmen have many more tricks at their disposal, including turning you over to a "closer," the sales manager or another salesman who'll give the negotiating screw a few more turns to see how much more he can wring out of you. As an ace bargain hunter, you can avoid all of these tricks.

The F&I Office

Your bargaining work isn't done once you've finally come to trade-in and price agreements and you're out of the sales room. Next comes the F&I office, where the financing and insurance is arranged. Your absolute best bet is to get your financing somewhere else, at your credit union or bank, *before* you hit the showroom so there's nothing for the dealer to negotiate. If you can't—or if the dealer's offering a special low-price finance package your bank can't match—then go for it. However, your anti-bargain antennae should be out and on alert, because you'll almost always pay more using dealer financing (traditionally about 2 percent) than going with an outside lender.

Avoid buying any sort of credit insurance from the dealer. Those nifty-sounding packages offering to pay off your car loan in full should you become disabled or die will cost you more in the F&I office than if you purchase them from your insurance agent.

Don't drop your guard yet! The F&I office handles more than financing and insurance. This is where they try to talk you into all sorts of options that you either don't need or can get cheaper somewhere else. Rustproofing, undercoating, paint sealer, and fabric protection are unnecessary in today's new cars and the dealer will charge you 80 percent to 90 percent above what they cost him.

If you want an anti-theft device, an upgraded sound system, or pin-striping, check prices from outside sources before you go to the showroom. You're likely to find much better rates on your own. So either go to one of those sources or get the dealer down to the same price.

Dealer prep charges are just what they claim to be—the *dealer's* prep charges. Don't pay his costs for him, and don't pay the *ADMU*, the additional dealer's markup that gets tacked onto certain sporty new models that are in high demand.

Car shopping online

If you'd just as soon pass up on all the fun and thrills of going head to head with the dealer but you still want a bargain on a new car, try shopping online. Several sites offer this service. You choose the make and model of the car you want, decide on an option package, and pick a snazzy paint color. Then your dream car configuration is sent to dealers in your area who e-mail you with quotes. You print out the one you like, take it down to the dealer, and buy the car. Some sites even help you get all that nasty paperwork going so you spend as little time as possible at the dealership.

The beauty of these car buying systems is that, because the dealer's provided you with a quote before you ever set foot on his showroom floor, the price-haggling portion has been excised. (Keep in mind, however, that you'll still have to be on your toes for add-on charges when you go to pick up the car.) On most sites the service is free, but you are expected to be on your honor and not click the "get quote" button unless you're seriously interested in buying.

Some sites offer a dazzling array of information in the form of articles, reports, photo spreads, stats, and side-by-side comparisons of various makes and models. Others offer financing and insurance links. Even if you're not in purchase mode, you can spend a lot of time road-surfing around in these sites constructing virtual creampuffs. Not clicking that quote button can be tough!

If you want to give Internet car shopping a spin, here are a few sites to get you started:

- Auto-By-Tel (www.autobytel.com)
- Cars@Cost (www.carscost.com)
- MSN's Carpoint (www.carpoint.msn.com)
- Priceline (www.priceline.com)

Over on the Priceline site, the folks who deliver the let-the-travel-agents-match-your-price concept for airline tickets have done the same thing with car buying. You choose a car, tell the site what price you want to pay or what sort of payments you'd care to make and then submit your "bid." Priceline then goes to work finding a dealer who'll accept your terms and notifies you within one business day when it finds one who'll play.

If it's successful, you pay a $25 matchmaking fee. Note that if you don't show up at the dealership to claim your vehicle, your credit card gets slapped with a hefty $200 "good faith cancellation fee." So if you decide to give this option a whirl, make sure you're serious.

Adoptable autos

Not everybody can afford a new car, and not everybody wants a new car. Sometimes going the pre-owned (used) route is a better option for a variety of reasons, price being probably the most important. A new car loses up to 50 percent of its value after its first birthday, so you actually get more for your money with a used vehicle.

Then there's the fact that, like computers, brand-new fancy cars tend to have more bugs than models that have been around for a while. It's sometimes wiser to let somebody else deal with all the factory call-backs for that first year or so, and buy the car after it's cut its automotive teeth.

For the die-hard bargain hunter, shopping for a pre-owned, private party vehicle is fun. Like shopping garage sales and estate sales, you meet a lot of people, get a peek at neighborhoods you'd never otherwise have investigated (or even known existed), and have the opportunity to turn up that truly magical buy that you can keep forever or sell later for more money.

B A R G A I N H U N T E R ' S J O U R N A L

• Winning the game •

When our friend Karl Kopf walks into the dealership to buy a car, he comes out with a bargain. His strategy? He tells the salesman what he wants to pay, no ifs, ands, or buts. If the salesman won't come to Karl's terms, Karl walks away.

During the Panama City Beach, Florida, resident's purchase of a new burgundy minivan, all negotiations ground to a halt when the salesman refused to honor Karl's price.

"I told you what I wanted to pay and this isn't it," Karl told the rep in no uncertain terms. "And then," he recounts, "I walked away. The salesman followed me saying, 'Come in and we'll make a deal.'"

"You make my deal or no deal at all," Karl told him. The rep agreed. They went back into the office, and the salesman wrote everything out, and then added $130 to the agreed-upon price.

"I see already you're figuring something different," Karl told him.

"That's just county taxes," the salesman said. "We can't ignore those."

"Yes, you can," Karl said.

The salesman said he had to consult with his manager.

> page 137

Restoration or resurrection

Adoptable autos fall into one of these five categories:

Cream puff. This is the one owned by that mythical little old lady from Pasadena, or the guy across town who's a perfectionist. Low mileage, no dents, no dings, immaculate inside and out, and meticulously maintained down to receipts for every oil change ever made.

Average vehicle. This one's owned by your Average Joe. Not a vision in clear coat, but defects that can be cured by a little TLC and the application of elbow grease. Probably needs a tune-up and a good detailing inside and out.

Fixer. Here's a car that can be worth a lot if you're willing to spend a little to make it right. May need a paint job, a new clutch, brakes, or a transmission. Use this defect as a bargaining chip.

Restoration. The weekend project—the quintessential 57 Chevy or 61 Mustang that needs new upholstery, new paint, some mechanical work, and industrial strength TLC, but has the potential to become a showpiece.

Resurrection. The lifetime weekend project—only for die-hard car fanatics willing to spend years of Saturdays hunting down no-longer-manufactured parts.

Treasure Chest Trivia

According to the U.S. Census Bureau, the average used car and truck on the road today is eight and a half years old.

The zippy speedster

The first stage in shopping for a pre-owned vehicle is similar to that of buying a new car from the dealer—you have to decide what you want and how much you're willing to pay. The easiest way to do this is to grab your local newspaper and turn to the auto classified section.

Vehicles are usually categorized by type—car, truck, recreational vehicle—and by year. Take a look at the kind of car you think you'd like and at different automotive years.

This will give you a quick guide to pricing in your area. If you had your heart set on a zippy red Speedster Sport Coupe, for example, but the ones in the paper are about $10,000 over your price range, you'll have to change your strategy:

- Choose a car with a similar sporty feel that sells for a lot less.
- Hold out for a Speedster that needs work.
- Wait for a seller who is desperate.

Keep in mind that you may wait a long time for the second or third options, so if you need wheels immediately, go with another model.

If there are only one or two ads for the car you want, check out the online classifieds, look up trade-in values on the Internet or library versions of the *Kelley Blue Book*. Some people have highly inflated ideas of what their vehicle is worth, so with only one ad to go by, you can't get a realistic idea of prices in your area.

Expedition Tip

Don't bother calling on ads where the seller thinks his beaut is worth a lot more than it really is. You can't get these people to come down in price. Save your bargaining skills for the guy who wants to sell at a realistic price.

Expedition Tip

Don't wait until your present vehicle has gone to auto heaven before you start shopping. You're in a much stronger position when you don't *have* to have new wheels immediately—you can afford to pick, choose, and haggle instead of taking the first thing that looks decent.

Runs better than it looks

Aside from the information value, the auto classifieds make entertaining reading. You can sometimes get a pretty good snapshot of the seller's mindset just by peeking between the lines.

BARGAIN HUNTER'S JOURNAL

< page 135

"Don't ask him," Karl said, "I'm leaving." And he walked out. Again.

But he didn't have to go far. The salesman followed him out the door and begged him to come back. He then wrote up a contract at Karl's price, including the county taxes. Karl won the battle.

"It's a game you play," Karl says. "Most people just want the car so badly that they fall for it. You have to be strong, even if you like the car. Otherwise you don't get your price. The dealer usually comes around."

Karl also advises seeking out the youngest salesman in the dealership. Why? Because he's inexperienced and doesn't know the game well enough to win.

One of our favorite ads read like this: *1989 Ford pick-up. Runs better than it looks. $1,200.* You can see right away that this poor thing is probably a wreck that you don't want unless you're looking for a workhorse to haul construction rubble. You can also see that the seller doesn't harbor any illusions about the truck. He knows it's in poor condition, leaving you to bargain your way to a nice deal.

Check this out: *1994 Cadillac DeVille, 54,000 miles, excellent condition. Lady-driven. $10,000.* This one could be argued two ways: If you're a man with an attitude that "women don't belong behind the wheel," you might deduce that being "lady-driven" is not a plus. Perhaps the car will have had the brakes ridden down to the metal, never had its oil or transmission fluid checked, or have dented bumpers from inexpert parallel parking. If you're a woman, however, you can argue that the car was probably treated with kid gloves. Its owner never burned rubber to show off, never cruised at 110 mph to see how it felt, and never hauled bags of cement in the back seat.

Sunday driver

When you've identified a vehicle you like that's in your price range, it's time to place a call to the seller and pre-qualify the car. Asking the right questions over the phone can save you a lot of time and effort. Unless you're merely looking for an excuse for a Sunday drive, this is a very important step. (If all you want is a Sunday spin, it's not fair to waste the seller's time—go find a new car lot and bother the dealer instead.)

Use the list of questions we've provided below. Some of the answers may be provided already in the ad, but it never hurts to ask. This will tell you if the seller is embellishing the truth about mileage for instance, or if he can't remember what he put in the ad, or if there was a typo (that terrifically priced Cadillac for $1,800 was actually supposed to be $18,000). It can also be a springboard for further insights about the car.

Car qualifier checklist
- Asking price?
- How many miles does it have on it?
- Automatic or standard transmission?
- Exterior/interior color?
- Overall condition?

- Any rust?
- Condition of upholstery?
- Any dents? Has it ever been in an accident?
- Is it mechanically sound?
- Does it leak or use oil?
- What kind of mileage does it get?
- Options (air conditioning, power windows, CD/cassette player, anti-theft system, cruise control, etc.)?

Is the seller the original owner? This establishes what in fine art and antique circles is called the *provenance*. If he is the original owner, he should know the car's history.

Why is he selling the car? This will give you an idea whether there's some hidden problem. People usually sell a car for readily apparent reasons, such as a family that requires a larger or safer vehicle, an elderly or deceased family member who's no longer driving, or (usually in the case of a fairly new car) payments that are too high. You'll have to use your bargain hunter's antennae here, but if the reason for selling doesn't sound quite right, put yourself on alert. "I can't afford to keep it up," for instance, is not the same as "I can't afford the payments," and could indicate that the upkeep (repairs) are an economic drain on the seller—and will be for you, too.

Honey or hellion

Once you've got these questions answered, you'll have an idea whether the car is worth further investigation. If it is, set up an appointment to view it. Here's your excuse for going out for that Sunday drive.

▣ xpedition Tip

Find out the wholesale and retail values of the car before you go take a look. It's one way to determine where to start bargaining if you decide you want it. You can go to the *Kelley Blue Book* or other car sites on the Net or check the information at your local library.

Many people dislike used car shopping because they feel they lack the skills to detect a lemon when it's squirting them in the face. It's true that you always run the risk of buying a bomb, but that can happen with a new car, too. In our experience—and we've bought a lot of pre-owned vehicles—most private-party sellers are genuinely honest folks who are as anxious to give you a good deal as you are to get one.

We're not mechanics and we don't profess to be. You should have any used car checked out by a reliable mechanic of your choice (not the seller's) before you hand over any money. But the following is a checklist of some things to look for on your pre-adoption visit that will help you ascertain whether you're looking at a honey or a hellion. If you call your mechanic—that ally you've already enlisted—and tell him you'll be bringing the car to him, he may point out other concerns you'll need to address.

The seller should be more than happy to let you poke around to your heart's content. If for any reason he isn't, you've got a strong clue that something isn't right and it's probably wisest to thank him for his time and split.

Car inspection checklist

- ✔ How does it look in overall appearance?
- ✔ Take a peek at the odometer. What *is* the mileage?
- ✔ Check for flaws in the paint. This can be a clue to rust or body repairs.
- ✔ Check out the upholstery. Is it torn or dirty beyond what a good shampoo can correct?
- ✔ Is the dashboard cracked?
- ✔ Look under the car. Are there fluids on the parking pad that could indicate an oil, radiator, or transmission leak? (If it's summer and hot, you may see air conditioning runoff, which is okay.) Hunker down on your knees and peer under the car. Do you see rust or bends where the frame may have been repaired after a bad accident? Are there holes in the exhaust system?
- ✔ Check out the alignment of doors, trunk, hood, fenders, and bumpers. If they don't line up well with the body, this is another indication of an accident that's tweaked the frame.
- ✔ Lift up the carpets and look to see if the metal is wrinkled, another telltale sign of an accident.
- ✔ Check the oil level. If it's low, it could be that the seller isn't taking care of the car as he should. The color should be relatively clear, never black, unless the car is a diesel, which turns dark quickly.

✔ Take off the oil filler cap. Is it clean? Water residue or a milky white appearance indicates a motor problem.

✔ Check the transmission level. It should be at the proper level, clear red in color and should not smell burnt or feel gritty.

✔ Check all other fluids: steering, brake, and clutch (if a manual transmission). They should all be clear—sludge in any of them means you'll need to have the car serviced soon.

✔ Look at the fan belts and water hoses. Do you see any hairline cracks?

✔ Check the battery. Are the terminals corroded? You should be able to tell how old it is by the date stamped on top, which indicates the year followed by the month.

✔ Inspect the tires. Uneven wear in front and back could indicate shock absorber or alignment problems.

✔ Have the seller start the car while you stand back and watch. Does it emit smoke?

✔ Does the car start right up or cough to reluctant life?

✔ Does it run smoothly?

✔ Check all lights, turn signals, sound systems, and other electrical functions including power windows, door locks, seats, sun roof, or convertible top. If it's a convertible, put the top up so you can check for tears.

✔ Test the air conditioning and heating units.

✔ Ask the seller to let you see any and all maintenance records, log books, and owner's manuals.

B A R G A I N H U N T E R ' S J O U R N A L

•Champagne, anyone?•

Ever have a private party car seller offer you champagne? We have.

Several years ago in Los Angeles, we went to look at a Mercedes 300-CD that was being sold by a young couple who had recently had a baby and wanted a family station wagon. They were asking $6,500, which we figured was about $500 under the car's retail value, so we went to take a look. We liked what we saw.

The car needed a new transmission, which we discovered when Rob detected a burnt odor to the transmission fluid, but otherwise it was in fine shape. Using the bad transmission as a bargaining chip, Rob offered the seller $4,000. The seller was shocked and said he couldn't take that little.

Rob countered with $4,500, claiming that the transmission would cost us $1,000 to $1,500. The seller said that was still not enough. So we thanked him for his time and headed toward our car across the street. But he didn't want to let us go.

"Wait," he called when we'd gotten no further than the curb. "Let me ask my wife." We stood in the driveway while he went into the

> page 143

Test drive!

If you're fairly satisfied with what you see, ask to take the car out for a test drive and take note of the following:

Is it a good fit? If you're a petite person, can you reach the pedals? If you're tall, have you got enough head and leg room? Will you feel comfortable on that long drive to Vegas or will you suffer a bad back before you've gone 100 miles?

Does it pull to the left or right?

Do the brakes work well?

Does it shift through the gears smoothly?

Are all gauges within normal ranges?

Does it make any strange or unusual noises?

Do you smell burning oil?

The one you've been waiting for

If you like the test drive, it's time to bargain. By the time you've gone through everything, the seller is probably convinced—or trying to convince himself—that you're a player. Why else would you spend so much time on his car? He's hoping you'll offer to buy the vehicle and will probably be very disappointed if you don't. In other words, whether he realizes it or not, he's ready to negotiate.

Let's set up a little scenario to show you what to say. You've just test driven the car you've had your heart set on. The seller is asking $7,000, which you know from your online research is exactly Kelley Blue Book wholesale. Retail is $10,000, so you knew when you saw the ad that, barring some horrible defect, it was a good deal. This is the one you've been waiting for.

It's an older model, but it's in pretty good shape. It needs new tires, a good detailing, and some minor mechanical work, all of which you figure will cost you a total of about $750.

The seller is anxious to make a deal because he's leaving for Europe in two weeks and he wants to get rid of everything so he can afford to rent an apartment in Paris. (Note: Be sure to ask if he's having a moving sale.)

You: I'm definitely interested in your car. You do have the title, right?

Seller: Sure, it's on the kitchen table.

You: Great. I'd like to give you $5,000 for the car.

Seller: I already have it priced below retail. I'd be willing to come down a couple hundred, but not $2,000.

You: I can appreciate that, but frankly, the car is not in perfect condition. It needs tires, a tune-up, a good detailing, and that's just what I see. I figure it's going to cost me at least $750 to get it in shape, and that's on top of the $5,000, which is really all I can afford to pay.

Seller: I'd like to sell it to you, but $5,000 is just too low. I could come down to $6,500, but that's the best I can do.

You: Gee, I'd like to meet you halfway but I'm still out the $750 to get the car in shape, and then I'll have to count in the money it'll cost me for sales tax, registration, and licensing. That's another $600 to $700 right there.

Seller: I really don't want to take less than $6,500.

You: I'd be willing to pay cash, which I have with me. (You show him a roll of bills.)

Seller: How about $6,000?

You: That's still steep for me. I guess I'd better go. It was nice meeting you. (You head toward your car at the curb.)

Seller (following you): I'd like to give you the car. You seem like a nice person and it'd be nice not to have to deal with it any more. How about $5,500?

You: I could manage that much. I'd like to have my mechanic take a look at it tomorrow morning, and if he gives it the thumbs-up, I'll take it.

Expedition Tip

When you buy a used car, go over the title carefully. Check that the vehicle

B A R G A I N H U N T E R ' S J O U R N A L

< page 141

house. A few minutes later, he came back out. "I'm sorry," he said, "but my wife says we have to take $6,000."

"That's more than we're willing to spend," Rob countered. "Thanks anyway." We started toward our car again.

"Let me talk to my wife," the fellow suggested. We agreed and waited again—no strain, since it was a balmy California winter day—while he went in for a consultation.

When he returned, he suggested $5,500. Rob held fast to $4,500. The seller came down to $5,000. Rob repeated our offer of $4,500. The seller went into the house to speak with his wife yet again. This time when he came out he offered us a magnum of champagne if we'd please take the car for $5,000.

We politely declined and headed for our car. He let us cross the street before calling us back to accept our offer (but no champagne, though).

We got the transmission fixed for the $1,000 we'd estimated and drove that car not only cross country to our home in Florida, but for two trouble-free years before selling it for $6,000—$1,500 more than we'd paid for it.

ID number (VIN) matches the one inside the windshield. Make sure the seller signs in the proper place and fills out any necessary fields. Motor vehicle department personnel can be extremely cranky about this sort of thing and it's no fun having to track down the seller after you've driven away with the car, especially if either of you leaves town.

Marks the Spot

If you prefer the no-haggle method, you can buy used cars online through most of the same sites that sell new vehicles. If you like the face-to-face encounter but don't see anything intriguing in your local paper and don't mind a drive to another area, try the online classified ads.

CHAPTER EIGHT # The Castle Keep

eing master or mistress of your own castle is part of the American dream. For most people, it's the biggest purchase of their lives and a giant step in terms of spending power and financial debt, so it can be both exhilarating and scary. How do you find a dream instead of a money pit? How do you negotiate so it doesn't cost the proverbial arm, leg, and head of hair?

Purchasing that private castle or commercial property is like any other form of bargaining—it just takes more money and patience. Property deals may sometimes be made in heaven but they're not generally made overnight. When you're spending a small fortune, you want the time to consider your strategy and think through your options. Whether your goal is to become a Trump-like mogul or just king of your own keep, you can do it!

Estates and keepers

Real estate purchases generally fall into one of five categories. Your strategy for shopping and for bargaining is the same, no matter which option is your goal. But it's important to decide which one you want—if you don't focus, if you're all over the hypothetical map, you can't do the research you need to find the right property and make that super deal. So as a very first step, choose a category:

The private estate. The reason most people buy real estate—as a home base, a haven, a tax savings, a place to decorate without getting a landlord's permission, and of course, a castle where you and not your landlord reign supreme.

The feudal estate. Having your own home and earning money, too, by buying a duplex or other multi-family property you rent out.

The turnover. The property—distressed, neglected, or ignored—that you buy to fix up, then sell to somebody else. (Some occupy their property while the work is going on, which can be either an adventure or a trial, depending on how picky you are about drywall dust, how long you plan to take before turning it over, and how often you want to move.)

The keeper. Investment property you purchase to keep, not as a residence, but as an income-earner for the long haul. This can be a single-family home, a duplex or four-plex, or an entire apartment building you rent out.

The business. If you're an entrepreneur, you may be looking for business property—a hotel, restaurant, office building, warehouse, or whatever suits your needs.

Once you've decided on the type of property you want to buy, the search is on. For the sake of expedience, we're going to refer to everything as a house or home, but you'll use the same bargain hunting techniques whether you're looking for a cozy condo, an apartment building, a coffee bar, or a corner store.

Expedition Tip

Like buying a car, buying a house is easier if you don't absolutely have to have one overnight. Start shopping when the need begins to make itself known, not when you're up against the wall.

The 3 ultimate rules

When you purchase that pair of jeans or jar of marmalade, you don't lose all that much if it turns out you goofed, but with property, your investment is magnified by thousands. Just like buying a car, doing the proper research is vital to getting a good deal. Here are the Three Ultimate Rules of Real Estate Shopping:

Rule #1: Know your market. When you set out to purchase a piece of New York City or Northbrook, Illinois, or wherever it is you've targeted, you need to understand the market. Is real estate in the area in a slump or an all-time high? How long has it been that way? Are changes glimmering on the horizon?

If prices are depressed, you've got a good chance of picking up a bargain, but only if the market is about to make an about-face. Just because it's cheap, there's no point in buying a little bungalow in an inner city community that's been on a downhill slide for years and shows no signs of turning around. If you find a cute but neglected cottage in a low-priced urban area that shows all the earmarks of becoming a trendy district (new boutiques, coffee houses, and bookstores popping up, for instance), then buy while prices are still low.

On the other hand, if there's a land boom in progress with everybody buying everything in sight, you can consider fair market value a steal. Don't expect to buy that same cottage for pennies after the neighborhood has completed its transformation and become *the* hot spot in the city. Land booms can happen out in the suburbs, as well. If you have your heart set on a property in a neighborhood where houses are snapped up as soon as they hit the market, you're not going to find a bargain-basement deal.

So how do you know what's hot and what's not? Ask your broker. A good realtor can give you an accurate picture of any neighborhood through his knowledge of the area as well as through reports pulled from the Multiple Listing Service (MLS). You can also determine a lot about a neighborhood through your own bargain antennae and—if you've lived in the area for a number of years—through your own observational skills.

E xpedition Tip

The majority of real estate agents belong to the Multiple Listing Service or MLS, a computer-based directory that gives prices, locations, and descriptions of just about every realtor-listed property for sale in the area. Make sure the realtor you choose is an MLS member—if he isn't, you'll lose access to hundreds of properties.

Rule #2: Location, location, location. Any realtor will tell you that location is everything, but a "good" location means different things to different people and for different reasons. For you it might be an outlook over a golf course; someone else might see such a locale as a constant rain of golf balls in their morning coffee. The big draw for you might be an outstanding school district for your kids, a breathtaking view, or a close commute to your job. (We know of one prospective purchaser who turned down a well-priced bay view condo because she could see her workplace across the water and didn't want to have to look at it in her off hours.)

Even if you think you're going to stay in the house you choose for the next 40 years, you probably won't. Lifestyles change along with age, family size, health, careers, and interests. When you look at locations, consider not only what appeals to you but what will appeal to potential sellers somewhere down the line.

If you can't afford a beachfront bungalow, a penthouse condo with a view of the city lights, or a mansion in Beverly Hills, you can still buy in an A-plus location. Choose a neighborhood where the residents have pride of ownership—where the lawns are trim, the houses freshly painted, and residents have added landscaping, decorative mailboxes, outdoor lighting, custom windows, and other features that tell you they're there to stay.

⊤ reasure Chest Trivia

Levittown, New York, is widely regarded as the first tract home neighborhood in the country. Built in response to the post-World War II housing rush, former G.I.s, their wives and baby boomlets could move into a two-bedroom, one-bath home with an attached car port for under $7,000.

Rule #3: Add value. This is the rule where your bargain hunting skills can really shine. Your ultimate goal in buying real estate—after scouting out a good location in a good market—is to locate a property where you can increase the value, just like when you buy damaged or demo merchandise at the retail store and make it sparkle. Find the worst house in the best neighborhood and get ready to make a deal.

As an ace bargain hunter, you've got an advantage over the average buyer. You've trained your eye and mind to pick out the treasure among the trash. When you look for real estate, here's what you'll seek:

Curb appeal vs. curb repel. Houses often go begging for a buyer because they need a simple beauty makeover. There might not be anything structurally wrong with them, yet they're multiple listing wallflowers. They don't get shown by real estate agents and they certainly don't get buyers because they've got peeling, flaking paint, sagging screens and gutters, and ragged lawns. Or they're tidy enough but they've been painted in particularly gruesome shades of chartreuse and mustard by owners with a defective color sense.

Most people lack the ability to look at a décor-challenged house and see it as it would look with simple changes: fresh paint, new screens, a mowed lawn, and some flower beds. But *you* can, and therefore you've got a chance at a great deal.

Outmoded original. Some homes don't sell because they're old-fashioned, not in a charming, vintage sense, but in an outmoded one. They may have small, boxy rooms that are at odds with the open plans favored today, kitchen appliances that were trendy in 1954 but now appear antique, and bathroom fixtures that seem to have come straight from a downtown hotel for derelicts.

Again, the average shopper can't look beyond these basically cosmetic flaws to the terrific bone structure underneath, so a house like this sits on the market without a taker. This one will take more work than its lesser cousin that only needs paint and some gardening, but if you're a handy man or woman, or the funds can be allocated out, you can knock out a few walls, replace fixtures, and own a charmer purchased at a bargain price.

Motivation plus. If you're just not the fixer type—you end up with more paint on yourself than on the roller, and you and the business end of the hammer always seem to end up in awkward meetings—a bargain can still be found. Scout out homes where the seller may be motivated to take a lower price, perhaps one that's fallen out of escrow in a previous sale, or where the seller has been transferred and is in a hurry to leave town. Unlike the other types of homes in this section, you can't tell the "motivation-plus" from a "drive-past," but you can ask your realtor to be on the lookout. You'll often see ads that say "motivated seller."

E xpedition Tip

Don't confuse a fixer that needs only the renovation version of makeup or a nose job with the handyman horror that has structural defects. Falling foundations, perforated plumbing, bad wiring, and rotten roofing can add up to more woes than wonders.

Window shopping

Make real estate window shopping a part of your routine bargain-hunting expeditions. Even if you're not planning a move, it's smart to have a handle on which neighborhoods are hot, what prices are like, and what various dollar amounts will bring.

In supermarkets and restaurants, you'll find free publications like *Homes & Land*, which carries full-color listings of all sorts of properties in your area. You can also find scads of listings on the Internet, in your Sunday newspaper, and in shopper publications.

It's unfair to present yourself to a real estate agent as a serious buyer when you're just browsing, but there's nothing wrong with stopping in at open houses. (In fact, bored realtors will probably welcome your company. And you can tour model homes as often as you like.)

The beauty of property window shopping, of course, is that you never know when that serendipitous perfect house will appear. Because you'll have been researching the market all along, you'll recognize it and be ready to buy.

Treasure Chest Trivia

In real estate lingo, a *FSBO* (pronounced fizbo) is a house that's *for sale by owner*.

The genie in the realtor's jacket

Buying real estate is different from buying a pair of Reeboks or a refrigerator in one important aspect: the broker. On most bargain adventures, you go one-on-one against the seller. In property transactions, you choose a real estate agent to act as a liaison between you and the seller. This person plays a very important role in the entire process, acting as your negotiating proxy, expressing your ideas and emotions to the seller and his agent, and advising you along the way.

Some people believe an agent is an unnecessary part of the equation, and in some cases this is true. However, a good real estate broker can be well worth his or her commission, and unless you really understand the market, the neighborhood, the mechanics of the process, and the seller, your best bet is to cheerfully enlist the broker's assistance.

How do you find that genie in a realtor's jacket and build the kind of relationship that will bring you a super deal? First you have to identify the kind of realtor you want—an expert who knows the market in your town and in the neighborhood you've targeted inside and out. You'll need an individual who knows all the tricks of the trade, who's been in real estate long enough to understand the fine points of negotiating deals, and who can work with mortgage brokers, banks, escrow officers, and appraisers. In essence, one whose personality suits your own.

Not everybody's an expert just because they have a real estate license. There are lots of agents out there who are at it part-time because it seems like a good way to earn money and isn't an expensive way to launch a career. Because these people aren't relying on real estate sales to earn their livelihood, chances are they haven't devoted enough time or attention to become experts. Naturally, an expert is what you want.

There are also an awful lot of real estate agents swimming around in the property pool who have neither ambition nor imagination. Cross these folks off your dance card as well. Your agent must have the drive to help make your deals a reality and the vision to see what you see. If they can't, they won't be able to bargain effectively on your behalf.

The top producer

Now that you know what sort of agent you want on your team, how do you find one? Delve into the home buying publications like *Homes & Land* and dig out the Sunday real estate section of your local paper. These sources should give you an inkling of which agents seem right for you. Agents pay for their own advertising (unless it's an office-wide ad paid by the broker), so the ones who have larger ads are most likely to be the major players in your town. They've got enough sales to pay for the ads and they're ambitious enough to get out there and push properties.

Reading through all these ads will also tell you which agents are the top producers, the ones who've sold millions of dollars in real estate in the past year. (Actually, it's not the ads but the agents who'll trumpet this news—real estate people aren't shy.) Last but definitely not least, you'll discover which top-selling agents work the neighborhoods you've targeted—another important criterion for your real estate ally.

The appointment

After you've identified three or four top producers, call up one that seems the best and tell him what you're looking for: the neighborhood, the type of property, and the amount you're willing to spend.

Make an appointment to come into the agent's office and look through the MLS listings. Did the agent find the sort of houses you want? Are they in your price range? Do the houses the agent found require minor makeovers or major surgeries? Do your personality and the agent's mesh? Quiz them about their background and experience.

Naturally, if they haven't gotten the picture, thank them for their time and move on to the next agent. Unless you live in a very small village, you'll have lots of agents to choose from, so don't feel limited to the first few and don't get discouraged. Keep working at it and you'll find that gem.

Don't go out to view property with an agent you're not interested in, no matter how hard they try to convince you. It's not only a waste of both their time and yours, but the situation can become awkward if they show you a property you decide to buy through someone else later on. (Technically, your business on that property belongs to the first agent who shows it to you.)

What happens if you find the perfect property on your own without benefit of a broker or agent? Even if it's sporting somebody else's for sale sign, your best bet is to call your own agent, ask him to find out all the details, and then arrange for you to view it.

If you don't yet have an agent, you've got a choice. If your bargain hunter's instincts tell you it's a hot property and requires quick action, go with the listing agent whose name is on the sign. If not, go with the same steps explored above so you don't get stuck with someone who can't or doesn't want to negotiate on your behalf.

Broker or agent

What's the difference between a real estate broker and a real estate agent? A broker is an agent who has taken extra courses and undergone more extensive testing to become certified as a sort of "master agent." An agent has to work under a broker's supervision, but a broker can be a one-person office if he likes.

Some experts recommend working only with brokers, reasoning that their greater knowledge makes them more qualified to wheel and deal. Some brokers are indeed sharper than the average agent, but you can also find extremely qualified agents who are happy working under someone else's shingle and just haven't taken the time to go for the broker's license.

Don't take one or the other as a plus or a minus. Do your own research and then decide which is the better ally for you.

House Hunter, P.I.

You've found the perfect agent and together you're going out to look at what just might be the perfect property. You'll want to do an on-site inspection, just as you do when you buy that pre-owned car and you'll want to sound out the seller if he's home. Think like a private eye and find out as much as you can before you get there—the more detective work you do, the better idea you'll have of what to expect and what to look for. Ask your agent these questions:

How long has the property been on the market? If it's been listed for a long time (and the market is not so depressed that this is the norm), there's a reason:

The price could be unrealistically high, which may or may not be a good thing. If the seller is a stick-in-the-mud who's not particularly motivated, he's not likely to budge. If he's getting really tired of having his house up for sale, you might be able to convince him to come down in price.

The house could be cosmetically awful, so lacking in aesthetics that no one wants to make an offer. This is great for you!

It could be a house of horrors with major structural defects that previous potential buyers have already discovered.

It may have fallen out of escrow for reasons that had nothing to do with the seller, such as a buyer getting cold feet or unable to obtain the financing. Because people often spend their money before escrow has closed, the seller is probably highly disappointed, has put himself in financial hot water, and is in a frame of mind to accept another offer fast.

Has the house been shown often? If the house has received a lot of attention but hasn't attracted a buyer, it's probably priced too high for the market. Again, the seller may have had just about enough of holding open houses and keeping everything dusted all the time that he may be willing to lower his price—or he may insist on holding out. Naturally, as with all bargain-hunting, you won't know until you make an offer.

Have any previous offers been made? Some agents may impart this information if you ask (providing, of course, that they know the answers); some may not. If you can find out, for instance, that the seller already turned down an offer for $10,000 under his asking price, you'll have an idea of how low you can go.

Why is the property being sold? This is your best clue to the seller's motivation level. People sell homes for a variety of reasons that carry different amounts of negotiating weight.

Transfer out of area. This is often a good motivator. It's hard to buy a new house in a new town if you still have to pay the mortgage on an existing place, so taking less money to get out quickly is a reasonable option.

Can't make payments. Sometimes people get in over their heads on home mortgages. When the bank starts making foreclosure mutterings, these folks will often decide that it's better to take what they can get and pay off the note fast than to hold out for a profit at the expense of losing everything.

Death in the family. When an elderly parent passes on, the kids usually don't want the house—or the host of fresh memories that go with it. It's easier to sell at a low price and be done with it than to hang on for months in the hopes of a few more thousand dollars.

Divorce. Messy, but an unfortunate part of many modern lives. The bickering partners may decide to sell cheap to be rid of the house that holds them together.

Change in family size. Growing families often decide to go for larger digs. Because they're not pressured by circumstance to move quickly, they're not usually the best bet for bargaining—but you never know.

Already bought something else. People often buy a new house before the old one sells. If it doesn't move as fast as they've figured, they find themselves stuck with two mortgages—and often decide to sell for less to get out from under a problem.

◆reasure Chest Trivia

The top three reasons people move to a new home, according to the U.S. Census Bureau, are to establish their own household, because of the need for a larger home or apartment, or because of a new job or transfer.

Fancy vs. fixer

When you or your agent identify a potential property, have your agent pull up a list of *comps* (comparables) from the MLS. These comps will show everything in the neighborhood that's been sold in the last year or two, along with square footages, number of bed and bathrooms, and both the asking and sales prices.

This will give you a good idea of how the house you're investigating is priced. But put your common sense into play. Just because one house of the same size and style in the same neighborhood sold for $150,000 doesn't mean the one you're looking at is worth $150,000. The one that just sold may have been tricked out with fresh paint, new carpet, French doors, the latest appliances, and other fancy features. This doesn't make the fixer you're going to view with the flaking paint and the sagging screens worth the same money.

Unfortunately, sellers whose neighbors have bragged about their sale price often believe they can attain the same monetary heights. Or their real estate agent, who's anxious for the listing, tells them what they want to hear. So keep your common sense in place, your bargain antennae tuned, and be prepared to negotiate.

Exterior checklist

You've grilled your agent—you know everything it's possible to know about the seller and his motivation—and you're pulling up in front of your prospective purchase. Don't take off that private eye trench coat! Now's the time to exercise all your deductive skills.

Be prepared to take notes as you go through the house, using the checklists we've provided below, as well as anything else you see that strikes you. Just like when you buy a car, you'll use any negatives you see not only as "alerts" for potential problems but also as bargaining chips when you make your offer.

Keep in mind, too, that when you buy a house—just as when you buy that pre-owned vehicle—you should have a qualified home inspector go over everything before you sign on the dotted line.

✔ How does the house stack up against its neighbors? If you're going for a fixer, this doesn't really matter because you can give it curb appeal. If you're not, take a careful look. Is it the ugly duckling among the swans? Or is the whole neighborhood full of ugly ducklings? If so, tell your agent you're not interested. (Location, remember, is the key—if the neighborhood is in bad shape, it won't matter how many jewels you bedeck your purchase in. Its value will always be low.)

✔ Is the house uncomfortably close to a school (lots of kids running across the lawns and the sound of school buzzers resounding throughout the day), a fire station (sirens at all hours), a freeway overpass (vehicles rumbling past and smoggy emissions), or an electrical substation that poses a health risk?

✔ How does the house rate for curb appeal? A dog of a fixer on the inside can still have a charming exterior. This is a plus.

✔ How's the elevation? Is the house sitting in a hole that could represent flooding problems every time it rains? Does it sit above the crowd so water runs off instead of in, and provides a nice view, too?

✔ What about the approach? Does the house sit on a blind curve so that every time you pull out of the driveway, you risk vehicular mayhem?

✔ Is there adequate street and off-street parking for guests?

✔ Is the driveway cracked or pitted?

✔ Take a look at the roof. Is it missing shingles, tiles, or just plain worn out? If the area is prone to brush fires, is the roofing material fire-retardant?

✔ What about the fascia, the woodwork just below the roof? Does it show evidence of dry rot or water damage?

✔ Give the gutters a once-over. Are they falling off or even non-existent altogether?

✔ Are the lawns and landscaping overgrown and unkempt?

✔ Is the yard full of junk that will need to be hauled away?

✔ Does foliage grow too close to the house?

✔ Do you see any cracks in the exterior walls that could indicate foundation problems?

✔ What about retaining walls? Are they doing their job?

✔ Check out any decks, stairs, or railings for signs of wood rot or sagging.

✔ If there's a pool, what shape is it in? Is it heated? What is the condition of the heater (if any) and pump?

Interior checklist

Unless the neighborhood is bad or you've seen something to make you jump back into the car, reserve your judgment. Keep your eyes open and your mental gears turning—you've only just begun. Check out these interior factors:

✔ How's the floor plan? Is it open and friendly?

✔ Is the house dark or light and airy?

✔ Check out the ceilings. Are they low, making the house feel dark and cramped? Do you see water stains or other evidence of roof leaks?

✔ What is the condition of the flooring? Does it have carpets, hardwood, ceramic tile, or linoleum?

✔ Are there adequate electric outlets for each room?

✔ If the house is vintage, does it have circuit boxes or fuses that will need to be replaced?

✔ How's the plumbing? Check under sinks and around toilets for evidence of water damage.

✔ Is there central heat and air conditioning?

✔ Do you see cracks, bulges, or other evidence of foundation or settling problems in the walls?

✔ What appliances come with the house and are they in good condition?

✔ Are the air conditioning and heating adequate? What do the electric bills average?

✔ Has the house suffered any fire, flood, or storm damage, and to what extent?

✔ Does the house use city sewers or have a septic tank? Have there been any main line problems? What condition is the septic system in and how often does it get cleaned?

✔ Is there a homeowner's association? What are the fees? Are any assessments due or looming on the horizon?

✔ If the house is vintage, does it have an asbestos roof or flooring? (This can be a major cost to replace because of the all the special precautions necessary to remove and dispose of it.) Homes built before 1978 can also have problems with lead-based paint.

✔ If the house has a view that makes it special, how secure is that view? Can someone build between the house and the scenery?

The cost of turning an ugly duckling into a swan

If the owners are there, try to get a feel for the kind of people they are. Anxious or mellow? House proud or unconcerned? Easy to deal with or edgy? You'll want to go home and go over your notes. If you're not going the fixer route and everything seems to be in good shape, get ready to make your offer.

If you're looking at an ugly duckling, you'll need to determine how much it's going to cost you to turn it into a swan. Depending on whether or not you're not an experienced handy person, this can present some challenges.

Make another appointment to view the house, and bring along a friend, relative, or other ally who has experience and can help you make pricing decisions. If you've already made buddies with plumbers, electricians, painters, or other contractors, they'll often be happy to walk the job with you free of charge (or for a small fee).

Sit down with your list and figure out what sorts of things you can reasonably expect to purchase at the home improvement store (appliances, kitchen cabinets, bathroom vanities). Hit the stores and get prices on these items, then add them all up. The home improvement warehouse will be delighted to help you figure out your costs on materials and labor. (Figure in another 10 percent of your total material and labor cost as a contingency. No matter how well you calculate, there are always bound to be a few surprises.)

Playing the game

Now that you know how much you'll need to spend, you can formulate your offer. Let's say the house is listed at $150,000. The seller has found a new job and has already moved out of state. He had the house sold once but it fell out of escrow and it's been back on the market for three months. You figure it needs $20,000 worth of work to make it a swan. That takes the price down to $130,000. But you're a bargain hunter, so you want to get the price down lower.

You instruct your agent to offer $100,000, explaining that you feel this is a reasonable offer because of all the defects, which you list. Some agents may balk at this technique, feeling that a lowball offer only insults the seller, who'll retaliate by demanding full price and refusing to negotiate.

We've purchased many properties this way and you can usually work a deal. We've also sold lots of properties and had our share of "insulting" offers. You take it, leave it, or negotiate. It's all part of the game.

Make sure when you construct your offer that you insert two very important contingencies:

CHAPTER NINE Wrapping It Up

In and among all those shopping adventures, there also comes a time when, as they say in film-making, "It's a wrap." (Which the savvy shopper hears as "Wrap it up, I'll take it.) This is the moment when you decide to sell your stuff, make a tidy profit, and sometimes, give someone else a deal.

The 7 rules of resale

There are secrets to selling those bargains, just as there are to buying them. The quintessential advice, of course, is "buy low/sell high." You've learned through the course of this book how to accomplish the first half of the equation, but what about the second?

Follow along as we show you how to make the most from your ready-to-recycle merchandise with these seven rules of resale:

1. Know what you paid. You can only come up with a good sales price when you know what the item cost you. There's no point in selling something for $10 if it cost you $15. Make up a simple filing system and keep receipts for everything you buy so you can refer back when necessary.

For big-ticket items such as vehicles, it's important to keep a log of your expenses as well. Use a simple bookkeeping program like Quicken or keep a running tally, but add in everything that contributes to the cost. For instance, you'll want to start with the price of the car, add in the fuel pump and fuel filter you had replaced, those sheepskin seat covers, the custom dash cover, and even that clever driver's side coffee cup holder. Keeping a list has an added benefit: It shows the buyer how much you put into the car (bargaining chip for you) and demonstrates that you've added a lot to make it a good buy.

2. Know the value. The amount you paid is not necessarily the same thing as the object's value. You may have negotiated an absolute steal on something worth far more than the funds you handed over, or you may have paid a fair price at the time for a piece of merchandise that's not worth much today. So again, do your homework and determine the value.

3. Know the demand. Demand contributes a great deal to the value and price of a product. If you're selling vintage cuckoo clocks and everybody in your area is fixated on digital clocks, you'll have a hard time getting a good price. On the other hand, if you're selling lava lamps (which you probably couldn't give away five or 10 years ago), you can command a pretty penny.

4. Know how and where to market your merchandise. There are different markets for different goods. A 19th-century dining table priced to sell at $3,000 won't find a taker at a garage sale, while a 1985 kitchen set will be turned down by an appraiser from Sotheby's.

People in different areas of the country have different tastes as well. A nifty 50s Sputnik-style lamp that's all the rage in Los Angeles won't find a buyer in lower Alabama.

5. Know how to present your products. You'll get a better price when you "merchandise" your products. Dress them up and make them look like they're worth your buyers' money. When you sell a car, detail it. Clean and press old clothes. If you're selling small items like coins, jewelry, figurines, or even salt-and-pepper shakers, showcase them on a velvet background or a soft cloth. Make them look important.

6. Share what you know. Everybody appreciates honesty. When you buy a car, computer, or TV set, you want to know about any mechanical glitches. As a seller, it's important to provide your purchaser with the same truth. It's not only the moral and legal thing to do, but it helps establish a trust that can often lead to a buy.

For instance, when you point out that your antique nightstand has one wobbly leg that you never got around to mending, the buyer feels that you're honest and therefore the piece is quite likely to be as vintage as you say it is. He might be more inclined to pay your asking price—or close to it.

7. Set a price that leaves room for bargaining. It's not fair to highly over-inflate the price of your goods (and you run the risk of not selling them at all), but set them high enough that you leave a little room for haggling. You want to bargain when you shop, so give your buyer the same privilege.

◆ reasure Chest Trivia

Women spend more on apparel and services than men. According to a report by the U.S. Bureau of Labor Statistics, the average annual female expenditure is $660, compared to $425 for guys. The older you grow, the worse the spread. At age 65 and over, those expenditures are $407 for females but only $191 for men.

Treasure-selling venues

There are almost as many venues for selling your treasures as there are for buying them. You can't, of course, set up a booth at your local Wal-Mart or home improvement warehouse, but you've got plenty of other options:

- Hold your own garage sale
- Host a rummage sale to benefit a favorite nonprofit venture
- Take your goods to a consignment store
- Put stuff up for auction
- Place an ad in the local paper or shopper
- Sell at an Internet auction
- Post your products in the online classifieds

Glorious gift-giving

Another way to turn your bargains into someone else's treasure is by giving them away. It's been said that it's better to give than receive, and sometimes that's true. What doesn't contribute better to that delicious, warm feeling than giving someone a gift?

It doesn't have to be for a traditional occasion like Christmas, Chanukah, or birthdays. The very best gifts can be those given for no reason at all—delightful, serendipitous surprises that come from your heart instead of from the retailer's calendar of events.

We once found a set of refrigerator dishes—heavy pressed glass containers that were in vogue before Tupperware—and we wrapped them up in sheets of 1945 newspaper we'd discovered that featured the original advertisements. We put them in a box, decked it out in cheery gift wrap and ribbon and presented it to Terry's mom, who collects vintage kitchenware.

Bargain-hunting for gifts is a great excuse for buying while on expeditions, but it's also smart shopping. You can purchase not only spur-of-the-moment gifts but items earmarked for upcoming holidays and birthdays. When the Christmas crunch comes around or you've just remembered it's a colleague's big day, you don't have to rush out to the store. You've already got goodies on hand.

Designate a spot on the top shelf of your linen closet or in a bedroom drawer, and use it as your stash for future gifts. (The trick is to pick one place and stick with it—otherwise when holidays roll around, you've forgotten where you stored all that stuff.)

Really wrapping it up

Whether you're selling, buying, or gift-giving, bargain hunting is the way to go. But if you've read this book, you know this. (If you're one of those people who always reads the end first: Stop cheating! Go to Chapter One—you'll like it.) Bargain-hunting is the ultimate method for expanding your purchasing dollar, no matter what you're shopping for, and a terrific way to have fun while you're at it. Besides netting you a heck of a lot of good old capitalistic *stuff*, it also springs open the door to adventure, nourishes your creativity, and encourages recycling—one of the best ways to help our planet stay green.

Once you've got bargain-hunting in your blood, you're hooked for life. There are always new shopping worlds to be explored and new conquests to be made. You'll nose out fascinating nooks in every part of town and all over cyberspace, and turn every travel adventure into a bargain expedition as well. So get out there and get hunting! Keep your eyes and ears open, your sense of humor honed, and your bargaining antennae tuned, and you'll find those terrific deals in even the most unexpected places.

If you've got a nifty bargain adventure, tip, trick, or a snazzy way you've remodeled, redecorated, recycled, or reinvented a bargain-found purchase, we'd love to hear from you! E-mail us at **TRAdams@sprynet.com** or write to us care of Career Press.

Reference
Notes

Introduction

Page 15:
• National Retail Federation's *Stores* Magazine website, "Top 100 Retailers (chart)," www.stores.org. (©NRF Enterprises. Reprinted with permission).

Page 17:
• Statistical Abstract of the United States 1998, Chart #1223, "Appliances and Office Equipment Used By Households, by Region and Family Income: 1997." Source: U.S. Energy Information Administration website, www.eia.doe.gov.

Page 18:
• National Retail Federation's *Stores* Magazine website, "Top 100 Specialty Stores," www.stores.org. (©NRF Enterprises. Reprinted with permission).

Page 23:
• Statistical Abstract of the United States 1998, Chart #426. "Expenditures Per Consumer Unit for Entertainment and Reading: 1985 to 1995," Source: U.S. Bureau of Labor Statistics, Consumer Expenditure Survey (annual).

Chapter 1

Page 26:
• National Retail Federation's website, FAQs, www.nrf.com. (©NRF Enterprises. Reprinted with permission).

Page 29:
• Statistical Abstract of the United States 1998, Chart #1223, "Appliances and Office Equipment Used By Households, by Region and Family .Income: 1997." Source: U.S. Energy Information Administration website, www.eia.doe.gov.

Page 31:
• Interview conducted with Edward Allen Designs manager Vern Heywood.

Page 38:
• National Retail Federation's website, press release 3/15/99: "NRF Says Valentine's Day Will Flourish with Help From The Internet In 1999," www.nrf.com. (©NRF Enterprises. Reprinted with permission).

• National Retail Federation's website, 1998 Holiday Sales Data: "Holiday GAF Sales, 1988-1997" (chart), www.nrf.com. (©NRF Enterprises. Reprinted with permission).

Chapter 2

Page 49:
• National Retail Federation's website, "Historical Retail Sales By Region" (chart), www.nrf.com. (©NRF Enterprises. Reprinted with permission).

Chapter 4

Page 72:
• National Auctioneers Association website, "Discover Auctions!," www.auctioneers.org.

Page 81:
• National Association of Resale & Thrift Shops website, "Press Kit: Fact Sheet—The National Association of Resale & Thrift Shops and the Resale Industry," www.narts.org/htdocs/press.

Page 82:
• Goodwill Industries International website, "Goodwill Facts & FAQs," www.goodwill.org/about3

Chapter 5

Page 92:
• Statistical Abstract of the United States, 1998, Chart #165, "National Health Expenditures by Object, 1980-1996," U.S. Census Bureau, The Official Statistics.

Page 93:
• Statistical Abstract of the United States 1998, Chart #181, "Health Insurance Coverage Status by Selected Characteristics, 1990-1996," U.S. Bureau of the Census, Current Population Reports, p. 60-199.

Page 99:
• Statistical Abstract of the United States 1998, Chart #430, "Profile of Consumer Expenditures for Sound Recordings 1990-1997," Recording Industry Association of America Inc., Washington, DC, 1997 Consumer Profile.

Chapter 6

Page 113:
• National Retail Federation's website, "Retailing and Technology in the New Economy," www.nrf.com. (©NRF Enterprises. Reprinted with permission).

Page 115:
• Bloomingdale's website, "About Us," www.bloomingdales.com

Chapter 7

Page 126:
• Statistical Abstract of the United States 1998, Chart #1030, "Selected Motor Vehicle Indicators by Model Year 1992-1997," U.S. Bureau of Economic Analysis, Survey of Current Business, November 1997, American Automobile Manufacturers Association, Inc. and Ward's Automotive Reports, seasonally adjusted by BEA.

Page 130:
• Statistical Abstract of the United States 1998, Chart #1032, "Motor Vehicle Production and Trade, 1980-1996," American Automobile Manufacturers Association, Inc., Washington, DC, Motor Vehicle Facts and Figures (annual), and World Motor Vehicle Data (annual).

Page 136:
• Statistical Abstract of the United States 1998, Chart #1033, Motor Vehicles in Use 1980-1995, American Automobile Manufacturers Association, Inc., Washington, DC, Motor Vehicle Facts and Figures (annual), and World Motor Vehicle Data (annual).

Chapter 8

Page 148:
• Home & Garden Television, *Dream Builders*, Episode 102, "Levittown Revisited."

Page 154:
• U.S. Census Bureau website, "American Housing Survey, "Detailed Tables from the 1995 AHS-N Data Chart: Why Move?", Table 2-11.

Page 160:
• U.S. Census Bureau website, "American Housing Survey: Detailed Tables from the 1995 AHS-N Data Chart: What's It Worth?", Table 3-14.

Chapter 9

Page 165:
• Statistical Abstract of the United States, 1997, Chart #712, "Average Annual Expenditures of All Consumer Units by Race and Age of Householder, 1995," U.S. Bureau of Labor Statistics, Consumer Expenditures in 1995.

Bargain Hunter's Notebook

Pack the following pages
with all the essential shopping
and expedition equipment
you'll need.

They'll help you get organized and stay focused.
But don't forget the serendipity.

Half the fun of bargain hunting is in
the surprises you find
along the way!

Today's mission (things to concentrate on finding today):

_____

_____

_____

_____

_____

Measurements for current decorating projects:

_____

_____

Gift list (things to scout for friends and relatives):

_____

_____

Today's check-back sites:

_____

_____

Price matching or other comparison shopping research:

_____

_____

Brand name, model number, and description:

_____

_____

_____

_____

Notebook

Name of store or flea market/antique mall:

_____

_____

Space#: _____ Price: _____

_____

_____

Name of store or flea market/antique mall:

_____

_____

Space #: _____ Price: _____

_____

_____

Name of store or flea market/antique mall:

_____

_____

Space#: _____ Price: _____

_____

_____

Return trip reminder (merchandise to come back and bargain for):

_____

_____

_____

Name of sales ally: _____

Current price: _____

Date markdown expected: _____

Phone number: _____

Item: _____ Store: _____

Name of sales ally: _____

Current price: _____

Date markdown expected: _____

Phone number: _____

Item: _____ Store: _____

Name of sales ally: _____

Current price: _____

Date markdown expected: _____

Phone number: _____

Item: _____ Store: _____

Attach paint and fabric samples here:

Today's mission (things to concentrate on finding today):

_____

_____

_____

_____

_____

Measurements for current decorating projects:

_____

_____

Gift list (things to scout for friends and relatives):

_____

_____

Today's check-back sites:

_____

_____

Price matching or other comparison shopping research:

_____

_____

Brand name, model number, and description:

_____

_____

_____

_____

Name of store or flea market/antique mall:

_____

_____

Space#: _____ **Price:** _____

_____

_____

Name of store or flea market/antique mall:

_____

_____

Space #: _____ **Price:** _____

_____

_____

Name of store or flea market/antique mall:

_____

_____

Space#: _____ **Price:** _____

_____

_____

Return trip reminder (merchandise to come back and bargain for):

_____

_____

_____

Notebook

Name of sales ally: _____

Current price: _____

Date markdown expected: _____

Phone number: _____

Item: _____ Store: _____

Name of sales ally: _____

Current price: _____

Date markdown expected: _____

Phone number: _____

Item: _____ Store: _____

Name of sales ally: _____

Current price: _____

Date markdown expected: _____

Phone number: _____

Item: _____ Store: _____

Attach paint and fabric samples here:

Today's mission (things to concentrate on finding today):

_____

_____

_____

_____

_____

Measurements for current decorating projects:

_____

_____

Gift list (things to scout for friends and relatives):

_____

_____

Today's check-back sites:

_____

_____

Price matching or other comparison shopping research:

_____

_____

Brand name, model number, and description:

_____

_____

_____

_____

Notebook

Name of store or flea market/antique mall:

_____

_____

Space#: _____ **Price:** _____

_____

_____

Name of store or flea market/antique mall:

_____

_____

Space #: _____ **Price:** _____

_____

_____

Name of store or flea market/antique mall:

_____

_____

Space#: _____ **Price:** _____

_____

_____

Return trip reminder (merchandise to come back and bargain for):

_____

_____

_____

Name of sales ally: _____

Current price: _____

Date markdown expected: _____

Phone number: _____

Item: _____ Store: _____

Name of sales ally: _____

Current price: _____

Date markdown expected: _____

Phone number: _____

Item: _____ Store: _____

Name of sales ally: _____

Current price: _____

Date markdown expected: _____

Phone number: _____

Item: _____ Store: _____

Attach paint and fabric samples here:

Index

J

K

L

M

N

O

P

Q

W

About the Authors

Rob and Terry Adams live in Panama City Beach, Florida, in a house decorated and furnished with bargain-found materials and artifacts. As the managing partners of a real estate development company that buys neglected properties and administers beauty makeovers, they're always on the hunt for bargains of all kinds. They also spend a lot of time writing, and are currently at work on the fourth in a series of business start-up manuals.